# DAVID THOMPSON
## Fur Trader, Explorer, Geographer

# David Thompson

## *Fur trader, explorer, geographer*

### JAMES K. SMITH

"It is no mere accident that the present Dominion coincides roughly with the fur-trading areas of northern North America. ... We have given to the maple leaf a prominence which was due to the birch."

<small>H. A. INNIS,</small> *The Fur Trade in Canada*

Toronto OXFORD UNIVERSITY PRESS 1971

FOR MY FATHER
AND IN MEMORY OF MY MOTHER,
WHO WOULD HAVE BEEN PLEASED TO SEE THIS BOOK

The maps are by William Taylor

© Oxford University Press 1971

SBN 0—19—540180—8

2 3 4 5 6 — 6 5 4 3 2

Printed in Canada by John Deyell Limited

# Contents

# Illustrations

# Preface

In the interests of readability certain explanations and comments that would have interrupted this narrative account of David Thompson's life if they had appeared as footnotes have been tucked away at the end of the book. Hence there are two appendixes: one is on the Indian groups Thompson encountered; the other contains brief biographies of some notable men in the fur trade of Thompson's time. The sources for the quotations that are not from Thompson's *Narrative* are listed on page 109.

Again in the interests of readability, the spelling and punctuation in the extracts quoted from Thompson's writings have been modernized.

Lastly, in the two maps in this book, no attempt has been made to locate and identify the bulk of the hundreds of fur posts that existed — usually for very brief periods of time — in what is now western and northwestern Canada. Despite their grand-sounding names, each of these trading centres was little more than a rather hastily constructed log shack, which was often abandoned after one or more seasons of trading. Another complication is that many a trader built his post literally next to that of a competitor (or on the opposite bank of the same river) and gave his post the same name as that of his rival. Thus the maps identify only the principal depots and posts of the Hudson's Bay and North West Companies and those posts that David Thompson had particular reason to visit or those in the far west that he himself established.

# *Maps*

The Northwest (1798)

The Pacific Slope (1812)

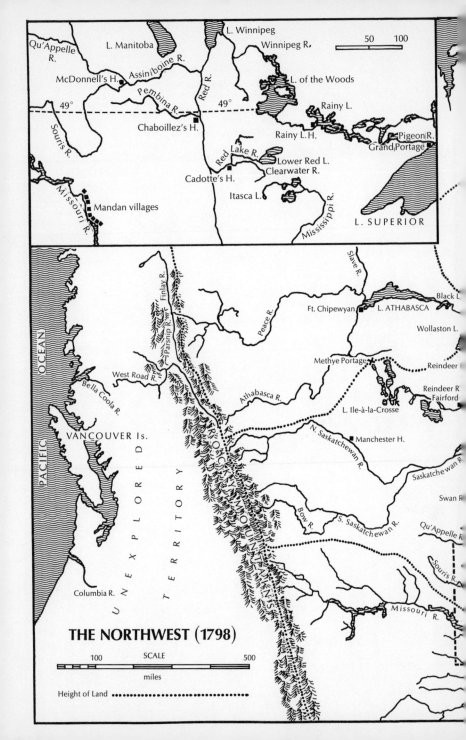

THE NORTHWEST (1798)

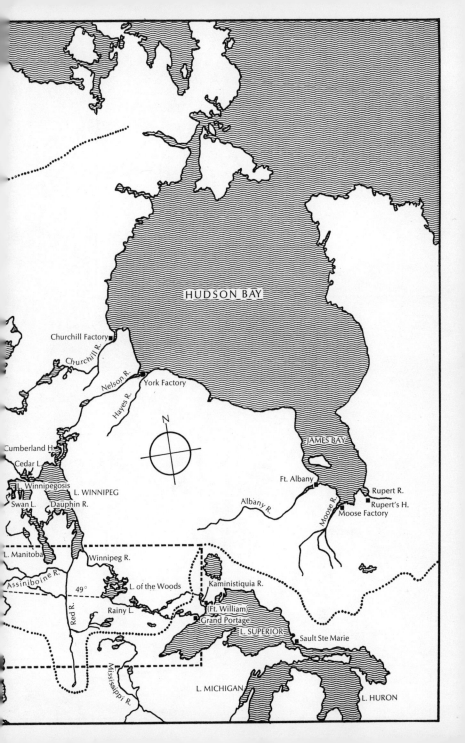

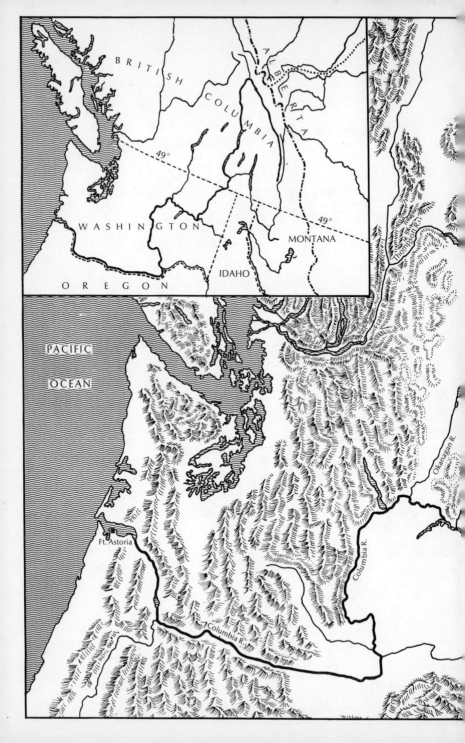

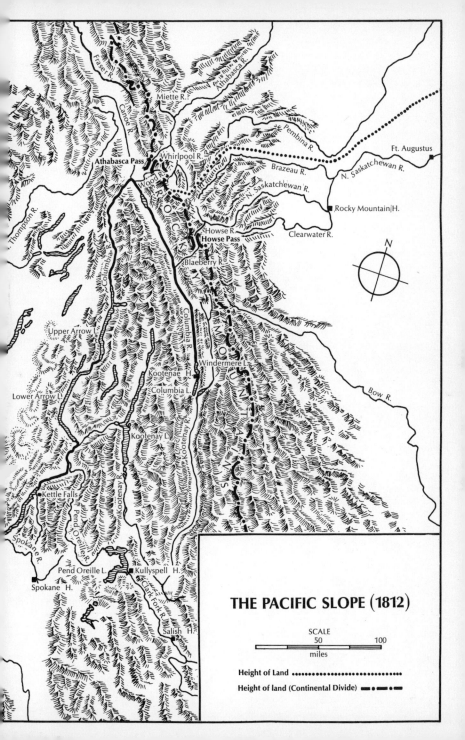

THE PACIFIC SLOPE (1812)

SCALE
50          100
miles

Height of Land ••••••••••••••••••••••••••••••
Height of land (Continental Divide) ▬•▬•▬•▬

# Introduction

In the summer of 1957 the Canadian government issued a five-cent postage stamp on which could be seen a map of part of western Canada, a buckskin-clad figure using a sextant, and the identification "DAVID THOMPSON 1770-1857". The stamp reflected the popular image of Thompson as a surveyor-explorer in the heyday of the fur trade, the man whose name is borne by the chief tributary of the Fraser River in British Columbia. Ironically the map showed this major river complex even though it was almost the only one in the Canadian West that Thompson did not survey; in fact he never laid eyes on it. Simon Fraser named the tributary as a mark of respect and admiration for the man who explored the headwaters of the Mississippi, which were not to be seen on the map. Nor did it show the Columbia River. Yet Thompson was the first man to travel and to chart its complex twelve-hundred-mile ramble to the Pacific Ocean.

David Thompson earned his living primarily as a fur trader. Despite the time and energy this consumed, in the course of twenty-eight years in western North America he managed to survey, plot, and map almost two *million* square miles of terrain as treacherous and hazardous as any to be found on the continent. He accomplished all this by such extensive travel and observation that, as late as 1915, many maps issued by the Canadian government, by railway companies and other agencies were based on the cartographic work performed by Thompson over a hundred years earlier. In addition he somehow found time to record a considerable body of information and opinion on natural history and anthropology. For sheer readability and descriptive power David Thompson's *Narrative of his Explorations in Western America 1784-1812,* based on years of daily notetaking, has few equals among explorers' journals.

Thompson was buried in Mount Royal Cemetery, Montreal. In 1927 a memorial service was held there, at which the principal speaker said:

*Without exact surveys and accurate maps, it would have been impossible to open and allot our western plains for the homes of our present and future millions, or to develop that vast land with roads and railways. Remembering this, we begin to realize the heavy debt of gratitude our country owes to David Thompson. He worked not merely for his employers but for the increase of knowledge, not so much for his own time as for the future.*

# 1

# An Apprentice and Clerk

*In the month of May 1784 at the Port of London I embarked
in the ship* Prince Rupert *belonging to the Hudson's Bay
Company as apprentice and clerk to the said company,
bound for Churchill Factory on the west side of the bay. . . .
It had been the custom for many years, when the governors
of the factory required a clerk, to send to the school in which
I was educated [the Grey Coat School, Westminster] to
procure a Scholar who had a mathematical education to send
out as Clerk, and to save expenses he was bound apprentice
to them for seven years.*

Thus begins David Thompson's *Narrative* of his explorations
in North America. Towards the end of 1783 the Hudson's
Bay Company had asked if the Grey Coat School could
"furnish them with 4 boys against the month of May next,
for their settlements in America". David Thompson proved
to be the only one worthy of consideration. He had always
displayed a talent for drawing and a special interest in geography; he also showed aptitude in mathematics. So this
fatherless lad with only seven years' attendance at a London
charity school behind him became, at fourteen years of age,
yet another raw recruit to the harsh, brutalizing, and often
dangerous way of life of the fur trade. It is unlikely that he
was even asked if he wanted to be shipped overseas. In

eighteenth-century England you did exactly as your betters decided, particularly if you were poor and without influential relatives or friends.

No portrait or sketch of Thompson is known to exist, but he is described by contemporaries as of small but sturdy stature, black-haired and snub-nosed, and with strong, home-ly features. Above all, he was quiet and observant. Almost forty years later, a young British doctor meeting him for the first time in Montreal described him in the same terms, remarking upon his simple, unaffected manner and innate dignity, and adding that "His speech betrayed the Welsh-man."

Churchill Factory provided a grim start for the new em-ployee. It was nothing more than a collection of log houses on the edge of a small bay five miles from the mouth of the Churchill River. All around lay the marshes and swamps of a bleak, subarctic land. Thompson arrived at the beginning of September; six weeks later the ground was buried in snow, and by mid-November the river was completely frozen over. There was so little wood for fuel in the region that the inhabitants of each log house were only permitted one fire in the morning and another in the evening. To keep warm between these times, if the weather did not permit shooting game, David Thompson paced up and down the guard room in a heavy beaver coat. Indeed the season was so cold that four inches of ice built up on the inside walls of the houses. And despite the twelve-foot stockade that surrounded Chur-chill Factory, savage storms drove snow against and over the stockade until drifts filled the entire post to depths varying from six to ten feet, forcing the inhabitants time and again to clear walkways from house to house. However, as Thompson was to discover, winter in western North America even at its worst was at least a change from the summer's heat and humidity, its ever-present mosquitoes, and the incredible number of fleas and ticks that infested prairie grasses and Indian encampments.

Writing years later in his *Narrative* of the time he spent at his first post, Thompson grumbled that he saw no need for his knowledge of writing and reading for his only business was to amuse himself "in winter growling at the cold; and in the open season shooting gulls, ducks, plover and curlews, and quarrelling with mosquitoes and sand flies", observing that "Hudson's Bay is certainly a country that Sinbad the Sailor never saw, as he makes no mention of mosquitoes." But in the course of his first year in North America he began to acquire at first hand the details of a trade that existed because of a persistent fashion in men's hats.

Throughout the seventeenth and eighteenth centuries and into the first half of the nineteenth century, there was a steady demand in the capitals of Europe for beaver hats, a demand that ultimately became something of a mania. Society, whether royal or aristocratic, clerical or lay, rarely appeared in public without wearing a broad-brimmed beaver hat — plumed, bejewelled, braided or embroidered; high, flat or tricorne in shape according to the fashion of the moment. Even army and navy officers wore headgear made from beaver fur. To possess a beaver hat (or hats) was to proclaim one's membership in high society. Like an expensive sports car or a mink coat, it was a status symbol of its time. The beaver hat was also a clear indication of wealth. That great seventeenth-century diarist Samuel Pepys records paying £4 for one in an age when a much-sought-after architect like Sir Christopher Wren earned all of £200 a year.

There is a simple reason why beaver fur makes the best-looking felt. Like all fur pelts, that of the beaver is composed of fine inner hairs and longer coarse outer or guard hairs. However, unlike almost every other pelt, each of the closely knit, silky inner hairs of beaver fur is covered with microscopic barbs or scales that overlap, thus retaining much body heat. Pressed together with steam or hot water, stiffened with shellac, and then rolled or beaten, these hairs mat together perfectly to form the finest, most lustrous felting. And the most desirable beaver pelts were those secured during the winter months when furs were longer, denser, and richer in colour. Although beaver dominated the fur trade from the beginning, it was not the only furred animal that was trapped. Such pelts as otter, muskrat, ermine, fox, lynx, mink, fisher, and marten were accepted by traders, and even bear and wolf skins had a modest market value.

As a young apprentice, Thompson learned about the habits of the beaver — a harmless, amphibious, woodland mammal with considerable construction skills. The animal's very ability to build a dam (to ensure a supply of water) and a large, conspicuous lodge made it easy for Indian hunters to find and kill the beaver after they had obtained European tools and weapons.

---

*RIGHT The beaver hat first became a common headgear among the wealthy in the late sixteenth century. Shortly afterwards brims were much broadened and hung down noticeably. However, the inconvenience of this wide flapping edge, which was most evident in cavalier times, led to the turning up of first one and then two flaps, until in the very early eighteenth century a third flap was turned up, which ultimately led to the creation of the cocked hat or "Continental". As can be seen, this altered brim remained in fashion in one form or another for many years. And, of course, hats with upturned brims are still common today.*

CLERICAL.
(Eighteenth Century)

"CONTINENTAL"
COCKED HAT.
(1776)

(THE WELLINGTON.)
(1812)

(THE PARIS BEAU.)
(1815)

"NAVY"
COCKED HAT.
(1800)

ARMY. (1837)

(THE D'ORSAY.)
(1820)

(THE REGENT.)
(1825)

*Formerly beavers were very numerous [Thompson wrote].*
*The many lakes and rivers gave them ample space, and the*
*poor Indian had then only a pointed stick shaped and hard-*
*ened in the fire, a stone hatchet, spear, and arrowheads of the*
*same. Thus armed he was weak against the sagacious beaver*
*who on the banks of a lake made itself a house of a foot*
*thick or more composed of earth and small flat stones,*
*crossed and bound together with pieces of wood, upon which*
*no impression could be made but by fire. But when the*
*arrival of the white people had changed all their weapons*
*from stone to iron and steel and added the fatal gun, every*
*animal fell before the Indian . . . the beaver became a desir-*
*able animal for food and clothing and the fur a valuable*
*article of trade; and as the beaver is a stationary animal, it*
*could be attacked at any convenient time in all seasons . . .*

*For the furs which the natives traded, they procured from*
*the French axes, chisels, knives, spears, and other articles of*
*iron, with which they made good hunts of fur-bearing anim-*
*als . . . Thus armed the houses of the beavers were pierced*
*through, the dams cut through, and the waters of the ponds*
*lowered or wholly run off and the houses of the beaver and*
*their burrows laid dry, by which means they became an easy*
*prey to the hunter.*

The Indians skinned the beaver and scraped the skin to
loosen the deep roots of the guard hairs. Skins might be
delivered to Hudson's Bay Company posts in pelt form —
*castor sec* — or as *castor gras*, cloaks or robes made by cutting
skins into rectangles and sewing them together with animal
tendons. These were greatly prized in the trade because,
having been worn by the Indians, the cloaks had lost most of
their guard hairs and the soft inner fur was exposed. A good

beaver hat was never less than three parts castor gras to one of castor sec.

The first recorded instance of the trading of furs in North America goes all the way back to July 7th, 1534, when Jacques Cartier, on his first known voyage to the continent, encountered two parties of Indians in the Gulf of St. Lawrence:

*They held up some furs of small value, with which they clothe themselves. We likewise made signs to them that we wished them no harm and sent two men on shore to offer them some knives and other iron goods, and a red cap to give to their chief. Seeing this, they sent on shore part of their people with some of their furs; and the two parties traded together. The savages showed a marvelously great pleasure in possessing and obtaining these iron wares and other commodities, dancing and going through many ceremonies and throwing salt water over their heads with their hands. They bartered all they had to such an extent that all went back naked without anything on them; and they made signs to us that they would return on the morrow with more furs.*

The Indian was quick to recognize the desirability of the iron tools and utensils he obtained from the French over stone or wooden ones. Yet his constant and often careless use of metal implements wore them out or broke them and forced him at more or less regular intervals to replace them. Similarly a gun obtained by barter almost totally replaced the bow and arrow, but with little idea of how to maintain a firearm the Indian was forced to seek frequent repairs or buy another one, and to purchase constant supplies of powder and ammunition. Other tastes the Indian — and his wife —

had acquired from French traders were for such items as liquor, tobacco, beads, shawls, thread, awls, silk and cotton handkerchiefs, fish hooks, and twine. The Hudson's Bay Company could offer all these and also such bulky or heavy goods as axeheads, hatchets, guns and shot, copper or brass kettles, woollen clothing and blankets, and traps — things that the French, in their frail birchbark canoes, had been unable to bring upcountry from Montreal in any quantity and that drew many Indians down to Hudson Bay to trade. "The principal things necessary for the support of an Indian and his family", one HBC trader noted, "and which they usually trade for, are the following: a gun, a hatchet, an ice chisel, Brazil tobacco, knives, files, flints, powder and shot, a powder horn, a bayonet, a kettle, cloth, beads and the like". He might have added that there was also a heavy demand for woollen clothing and blankets. Deerskin was a satisfactory covering in a dry, cold winter period; but when there was rain or sleet, clammy wet skins were not ideal garments, whereas wool kept its shape and dried out easily.

There is a popular impression that all fur traders defrauded the Indians by guile or with liquor. On many occasions this was certainly the case. But Thompson himself witnessed the tremendous appeal of European manufactures:

*The goods taken were of small value in money but of great utility to the Indians; everything is carried on by barter profitable to both parties but more so to the Indian than to us. We took from them furs of no use to them and which had to pass through an immense distance of freight and risks before they could be sold in the market of London. See the wife of an Indian sewing their leather clothing with a pointed, brittle bone or a sharp thorn and the time and trouble it takes. Show them an awl or a strong needle and they will gladly give the finest beaver or wolf skin they have to purchase it. When the tents remove, a steady careful old man or two of them are entrusted with the fire, which is carried in a rough wooden bowl with earth in it and carefully led to the place of the camp ... A flint steel saves all this anxiety and trouble. Iron heads for their arrows are in great request but above all guns and ammunition.*

The Company issued trade "tokens" to an Indian bartering furs in order to show him their value in relation to the goods he could select. Various HBC posts used different materials as tokens at different times — musket balls, porcupine quills, ivory disks, and numbered or grooved sticks of wood. (In the Arctic, the Company now uses aluminum tokens based on Canadian money, the unit of trade being the arctic white fox.) Whatever the form, one whole token represented one "Made Beaver", meaning the skin of an adult male beaver in "prime" condition — that is, killed between early November and mid-April. In other words the beaver was the unit of currency. For instance one winter-prime adult beaver pelt usually had the trade value of the following hides:

| | |
|---|---|
| 3 martens | 2 deer |
| 1 fox | 1 fisher |
| 1 moose | 1 bear cub |
| 1 wolverine | 1 lynx |
| 8 muskrats | |

(A silver fox, white fox, or otter was equal to two beavers, and a large black bear or a black fox equalled four beavers.)

So whether an Indian brought in beaver or any other kind of

pelt to an HBC post, fort, factory or house, he usually
bought a gun for the value of about twelve made-beaver, a
woollen blanket for eight, a knife for two, an axe or a pound
of beads or two pounds of shot for one made-beaver. (The
trade in pelts was so profitable that in 1676, six years after
its founding, the Hudson's Bay Company exported to the
Bay merchandise valued at £650 and imported £19,000
worth of furs.) As clerk and, on occasion, storekeeper, all this
was Thompson's early business education at Churchill Factory and farther south on the Bay at the Company's principal
trade depot, York Factory, where he went in 1785.

In 1786 Thompson was sent from York to the western
interior, equipped by the Company with the customary
"trunk, a handkerchief, shoes, shirts, a gun, powder, and a tin
pot." (The tin pot was his drinking cup.) He travelled up the
Hayes River to Lake Winnipeg and then on to the shallow,
brown waters of the great waterway of the northern prairies,
the Saskatchewan River, as clerk or writer to Mitchel Oman,
a Company servant. Thompson describes Oman as "without
education, yet of a much superior mind to most men, curious
and inquisitive, with a very retentive memory . . . much respected by the Indians and whose language he had acquired".
Oman, with whom he spent several months, taught him a
great deal about how to live, travel, and trade in Indian
country.

Thompson needed some of Oman's knowledge sooner than
he had expected. It was Company policy to send some of its
men to winter with plains-Indian groups in order to secure
their friendship and induce them to trap for furs. The next
year he was one of several employees sent southwest across
the prairies to winter with the warlike Piegan Indians. The
party travelled until "At last the Rocky Mountains came in

sight like shining white clouds in the horizon". On the banks of the Bow River, somewhere in the vicinity of the modern city of Calgary, the traders met about a dozen Piegans.

Again Thompson was fortunate. Where Oman had been his mentor the year before, this time it was Sarkamappee or Saukamappee, an aged Cree Indian living in the Piegan camp visited by Thompson and his companions. Sitting with the old man in his tipi almost every evening over a period of four months, the youth became absorbed in his stories about the Cree, most of whom lived north of the prairies in the forest country of river, lake, and swamp that lies in a broad belt between the Rocky Mountains and the region due south of Hudson Bay. Thompson made several shrewd deductions from Sarkamappee's explanations of his people's way of life:

*They bear cold and exposure to the weather better than we do and the natural heat of their bodies is greater than ours, probably from living wholly on animal food. They can bear great fatigue but not hard labour. They would rather walk six hours over rough ground than work one hour with the pick-axe and spade, and the labour they perform is mostly in an erect posture, as working with the ice chisel piercing holes through the ice [to fish] or through a beaver house, and naturally they are not industrious; they do not work from choice but necessity . . . the civilized man has many things to tempt him to an active life; the Indian has none and is happy sitting still and smoking his pipe.*

He heard of their kindness and courtesy to each other, the help and care offered to the sick, and the strong sense of communal sorrow felt at the death of any of their number. Thompson was impressed by the great care and tenderness with which children were brought up. They were seldom punished: it was the constant company and admonition of the old people that provided a child's early education. He noted too the simple Cree belief in the Keeche, Keeche Manito (the Great, Great Spirit), who left men and women free to arrange their own conduct but thoughtfully provided the earth, water, fire, and all the animals for mankind's comfort and use, provided that certain hunting rituals were scrupulously observed.

Much of what Thompson learned from Sarkamappee in the winter of 1787-8 gave him an early understanding of Indian habits, customs, manners, and religion that applied almost as well to the Piegan or any other tribal group he encountered as to the Cree themselves. Perhaps because he was himself deeply religious, he made copious notes on Indian theology and beliefs. At a much later date he wrote:

*All the natives of north America, from ocean to ocean, however unknown to each other and dissimilar in language, all believe in the immortality of the soul and act on this belief... They have no ideas of a judgement in the other world, with rewards and punishments, but think the other world is like this we inhabit only far superior to it in the fineness of the seasons and the plenty of all kinds of provisions, which are readily got by hunting on fleet horses to catch the bisons [buffaloes] and deer, which are always fat. The state of society there is vague, yet somehow the good will be separated from the bad and be no more troubled by them; the good will arrive at a happy country of constantly seeing the sun and the bad wander into darkness from whence they cannot return. And the darkness will be in proportion to the crimes they have committed.*

There is almost nothing in his *Narrative* to suggest that

David Thompson had a natural affinity for the mundane business of collecting pelts. On the other hand there is a considerable amount of observation of nature and man, from salmon to polar bears, from rocks fractured by freezing water to deposits of coal, from Esquimos and their way of life to that of many Indian tribes. He even describes the mouth parts of the "Musketoe" as detectable when viewed through a microscope, noting from personal observations with a magnifying glass that the bite we all feel is, in reality, two distinct bites that are so quickly done as to feel like one. The *Narrative* also reflects his ability to blend a keen observer's eye with a bent for mathematical calculation. It was these talents, together with a chance benefit resulting from a personal misfortune in 1788, that made David Thompson much more than a fur trader.

Late in 1788 Thompson was stationed at Manchester House, a Company post on the north branch of the Saskatchewan River. A few days before Christmas, while hauling wood back to the post, he stumbled and fell down the riverbank, breaking his right leg. The leg healed very slowly, and he had to endure a convalescence of a summer and winter downstream at Cumberland House, the principal Company post on the Saskatchewan. Here, during that winter of 1789-90, stayed Philip Turnor, the Company's surveyor, who gave young Thompson the training and impetus that launched him on his amazing career as a surveyor and geographer.

*This was a fortunate arrival for me as Mr. Turnor was well versed in mathematics, was one of the compilers of the nautical Almanacs and a practical astronomer. Under him I regained my mathematical education . . . and thus learned astronomy under an excellent master of the science.*

The pupil must have been exceedingly diligent because "by too much attention to calculations in the night, with no other light than a small candle", his right eye became so inflamed that he lost its sight for a time.

Thompson proved to be an excellent pupil for Turnor, who taught him all he was ever to know of mathematics, astronomy, and field surveying. The youth was instructed in the survey use of the telescope, the chronometer, the compass, and the thermometer; he learned to employ the sextant, the *Nautical Almanak,* and the artificial (mercury) horizon. That winter Thompson began to take a series of astronomical observations of the sun and stars in order to determine the exact latitude and longitude of Cumberland House. The position he ultimately assigned to the fur post — 53 degrees, 56 minutes, 44 seconds north latitude and 102 degrees, 13 minutes west longitude — is nearly identical to that which it occupies on any authoritative map today. In addition, late in 1789 he began to keep the first of many journals in which his prime daily entries were thermometer readings, notes on wind direction and force, and general remarks on the climate.

From 1790 until he left the West in 1812, David Thompson did almost as much surveying as he did trading. There was no river or lake he travelled that he did not survey and survey again if his journeyings took him over the same waters. There was no post, fort, or house where he stayed of which he did not plot the latitude and longitude, and if he went there again, he took fresh observations in order to verify his earlier figures. Indeed the series of astronomical observations he was able to make at individual fur posts were as a rule his most accurate work; when he was surveying on his travels he tended to calculate compass bearings only to the nearest five degrees and to estimate distances to the nearest quarter-mile by eye or elapsed time of travel. But Thompson was not concerned with pin-point accuracy. His goal was to determine the geography of a vast wilderness.

# 2

# *The Western Forests*

Thompson's apprenticeship ended in 1791 when he was twenty-one, and that year he received a letter from the Company's secretary in London offering him a contract for three years at £15 per annum. A salary and the status of servant or trained man were pleasant changes from simply being fed, clothed, and instructed in a trade. He was encouraged too by a statement in the letter that "every information that can tend to form a good survey and map of the country inland will always be particularly acceptable to us." In fact the letter stipulated his employment as a "surveyor and trader". However, there was little else to feel cheerful about. Thompson was working for the Company during a time in its history when powerful competition plagued the organization.

The first Europeans who made their way into the prime fur-bearing regions of what is now western Canada did so by two main routes. The bold *coureurs de bois*,* and later the restless trader-explorers who searched both for furs and the fabled "Western Sea" beyond the "Shining Mountains" that would lead to the riches of the East, kept moving farther and farther inland from one exploited beaver region to the next unexploited one. Thus they followed the rivers and lakes

* "Runners of the woods", individual fur traders who were refused — or did not bother seeking — the trading licences issued by the government of New France in its attempts to control, and to profit from, the trade.

leading north and west out of the Great Lakes-St. Lawrence watershed on to the great plains and then into the huge transcontinental northern or boreal forest, an immense region inhabited by millions of furred animals. Beginning in 1670, Englishmen working for the "Governour and Company of Adventurers of England trading into Hudson's Bay", a company granted sole trade and commerce in those regions whose waters emptied into Hudson Bay, built several fortified houses or trading-posts on the Bay and bartered for furs with the Indians of the western interior. By 1682 these posts, or factories as some were called, were Rupert's House, Moose Factory, and Fort Albany, all on James Bay, and Fort Nelson (later York Factory) on the southwest shore of the Bay where the Nelson and Hayes Rivers enter it. Company servants only occasionally explored the western interior from their posts because the English pattern of trade was always to entice Indian middlemen down to the Bay. Since the French shrewdly took goods to the western Indians and saved them the trouble of travelling to and from Churchill or York, it seemed as if the French would take over the fur trade of the West as they had that of the Great Lakes area. But the battle of the Plains of Abraham in 1759 delivered New France, and as it happened control of the fur trade, into rival hands.

The British (often Highland Scots) army contractors and merchants who flocked into Montreal in the wake of Wolfe's regiments took over the French fur trade in its entirety — language, transport methods and routes, trading customs — and caused the Hudson's Bay Company considerable loss of trade during the last three decades of the eighteenth century. Several of these Montrealers furnished the goods that independent traders took west to exchange for furs. Year by year, the number of traders grew steadily, and Indians soon reported to the Company that its rivals were "as thick as Musket-tos" in the area south of James Bay. By the late 1760s a number of them, with the geographical knowledge and help of French-Canadian voyageurs,* had made their way as far as Lakes Winnipeg and Winnipegosis, and one of them, James Finlay, did extremely well bartering for furs 150 miles west of the outlet of the Saskatchewan into Lake Winnipeg. Fin-lay, a canny Scot, had also left men with several canoe loads of powder, shot, muskets, trinkets, tobacco, and rum at two other points where they could intercept Indians going down to the Bay. In the early 1770s another Scot, Thomas Corry or Curry, established a trading post at Cedar Lake, near the mouth of the Saskatchewan, and made so much money in two winters of trading that he was able to set himself up in a business when he returned to Quebec.

Such success astounded the Montreal fur merchants — or agents, as they termed themselves — and galvanized them into subsidizing greater trading activity. By 1774 their partners, the traders who wintered in the west, had so reduced the flow of furs to Churchill and York that the Hudson's Bay Company was forced to send Samuel Hearne, one of its most experienced officers, to found Cumberland House on an island in the Saskatchewan. This post was used to check the operation of the Montrealers along the river and to prevent the Indians of the Churchill River country from being enticed south to trade with the Montrealers. By the time Thompson joined the Company, although the preference was still to draw Indians down to the Bay posts, HBC men were begin-ning to take trade goods inland.

By 1775 some of the Montreal agents were beginning to

---

* Canoemen from Quebec who paddled and portaged or hauled trade goods over the numerous portages alongside rapids or connecting nearby rivers and lakes.

realize that they would have to pool their capital in groups in order to offset the enormous costs and frightful risks of transporting trade goods across 2000 miles of wilderness in frail birchbark canoes and then returning the following year over the same lakes, portages, and rivers raging with spring runoff. In addition they wanted to penetrate farther up the Saskatchewan and its northern branch and cut off the Cumberland House-York Factory trade closer to its source. But an even longer supply route from Montreal demanded more money and increased the risks. Thus it was about this time that the North West Company, as a group of agents were already calling themselves, began to emerge as a loose but powerful coalition of fur interests. In the course of the winter before David Thompson arrived at Churchill Factory, these Nor'Westers worked out a reorganization that for a time was to give them something close to a monopoly of the fur trade and enabled them to create a business complex that stretched north into Arctic regions and as far west as the Pacific coast. They have been strikingly described by W. Stewart Wallace:

*The story of the Nor'-Westers, though not without its darker pages, is a brilliant chapter in the history of Canada. No braver or more picturesque band of adventurers ever put it to the touch, to gain or lose it all. Some of them were French Canadian traders and voyageurs, the sons of those who had followed La Vérendrye to the rivers and prairies of the West in the dying days of the French regime. Others were American frontiersmen who had served their apprenticeship in the fur-trade in the valleys of the Ohio and the Mississippi. Most of them were Scottish Highlanders, the sons of those who had come to Canada in Wolfe's army or as*

*United Empire Loyalists in the American Revolution. The
number of them who were connected with that gallant regi-
ment, the 78th or Fraser's Highlanders, is remarkable; and it
is no less remarkable that of the numerous Frasers, McTav-
ishes, and McGillivrays, who played such an important part in
the history of the North West Company, nearly all came from
Lord Lovat's estates [in the north of Scotland]. The names
of the North West Company partners sound like a roll-call of
the clans at Culloden. These men were hardy, courageous,
shrewd, and proud. They spent a good part of their lives
travelling incredible distances in birch-bark canoes, shooting
rapids, or navigating inland seas. They were wrecked and
drowned. They suffered hunger and starvation. They were
robbed and murdered by the Indians, and sometimes by one
another. They fell the victims of smallpox, syphilis, and rum.
Yet they conquered half a continent, and they built up a
commercial empire, the like of which North America at least
has never seen.*[1]

The men from the Bay contemptuously referred to their
rivals as the "Pedlars from Quebec" because they always took
goods to the Indians and haggled with them for furs, but
their disdain was foolish and ignored some hard facts. The
Nor'Westers were very aggressive competitors; they cut prices
to steal away old HBC customers and ranged deeper into the
wilderness to intercept others or to find new sources of
supply. These traders were such astounding opportunists that
in 1794 Thompson was not very surprised to observe one
building his fur post a mere thirty yards to the east of where
he himself was still busy constructing his. A number of
Nor'Westers had no scruples about beating up customers on
suspicion of trading with the Company, and many of them in

effect controlled groups of Indians by making them dependent upon handouts of liquor.

More importantly, despite the Company's inexpensive sea route to the threshold of the western fur country, in contrast to the Montrealers' 2000-mile haul to reach the same region by 1791 the Nor'Westers had not only bypassed Cumberland House and established several posts on the North Saskatchewan, but they were well established a further 1000 miles to the north and west in that Eldorado of the fur trade, the subarctic Athabasca region, where winter lengthened to eight or nine months of the year and where furs were correspondingly heavy, rich, and glossy. In 1776 the enterprising Alexander Henry (the Elder) and two of the aggressive Frobisher brothers, Thomas and Joseph, had been the first to hear about the rich peltry of Athabasca from Chipewyans they intercepted on their way down the Churchill to the Bay. In 1778 Peter Pond, a shrewd New Englander, had been the first Pedlar to enter the region; he worked his way west on the upper Churchill and then north over Methye (La Loche) Portage, a trail over a low, broad ridge that separates waters draining down to Hudson Bay from those running to the Arctic Ocean. When Pond came back "out" the following summer with 140 packs of fine, silky, beaver skins, he had had to leave more cached behind because he did not have the canoes to transport them. Those pelts were the first great bonanza in the Northwest, and it has been estimated that, in the years after 1779, half the huge profits of the North West Company were hauled over the stony, sandy soil of the twelve-mile Methye Portage.

The Athabasca region, which has been described as "four-fifths drowned and when not frozen is half-hidden by mosquitoes and black flies", was the source from which the

Hudson's Bay Company had long been accustomed to receive a large part of the supply of furs that were brought down to York and Churchill by Indian middlemen. Samuel Hearne reported in 1777 that, thanks to his practice of sending the Northern Indians (Chipewyans) "into the Atha-pus-cow Indians country to bring off their furs . . . the Northern Indian trade this year is upwards of 11,000 made Beaver, whereas formally [sic] it was never estimated at more than 6,000 on average." However, despite many warning reports from its servants of the Montrealers' successes on the Saskatchewan and "to the Northward", it was 1790 before the Company sent Philip Turnor to view the region and report on it. His findings in 1792 confirmed that the Pedlars had a virtual monopoly of trade at Fort Chipewyan. Turnor wrote that on Lake Athabasca the Nor'Westers had "the compleatest Inland House I have seen in the Country" with "a sufficient quantity of Trading Goods . . . for at least two years to come." He went on to report that:

> . . . the Trade of this Country this year is as follows

| | |
|---|---|
| Slave Lake | — 54 packs and much more expected: this trade is about half Martins |
| Peace River | — 150 packs little except Beaver |
| Athapescow Lake | — about 90 packs mostly Beaver |
| Athapescow River | — 25 packs mostly Beaver |

As it happened the price in made-beaver that the Nor'Westers secured for European goods was very high, and

The beaver was such an important trade staple that all merchandise was valued in beaver skins, and all other fur pelts were rated in terms of a beaver pelt. In other words, the beaver was the medium of exchange. It was the practice of the Hudson's Bay Company to issue trade tokens to an Indian bartering furs in order to show him the value of his pelts in relation to the goods he could select. A whole token represented one "Made Beaver" — the pelt of an adult, male beaver in prime condition. In 1854 the Company began issuing special brass tokens of the value of 1, 1/2, 1/4, 1/8 Made Beaver.

Above is such a token. On one side is the Company's coat of arms, and on the reverse can be seen the Company monogram, the initials of the district (East Main) for which the token was required, and the value. The initials "NB" referring to "Made Beaver" were incorrectly engraved by the die-cutter; this error was perpetuated and led to the belief that "Made Beaver" was sometimes called "Natural Beaver"'

Below is a North West Company beaver token. (The head is that of King George IV.) The Company's issue of "Beaver Coinage" was far less than that of the HBC. Today only a handful of these tokens are known to exist.

the profits were glorious. In 1780 the annual value of trade from the forests to the north of the great plains had been estimated by Montreal agents at £50,000. By 1790 their estimate of the Northwest trade — the western forests and Athabasca — was £100,000, almost half the total trade of Montreal and Quebec.

One result of Turnor's discovery was that in 1792, in the words of Joseph Colen, the chief of York Factory, "Hugh Leask and Peter Bower are appointed to go up Nelson River and accompany Mr. David Thompson to the Miss a nippe [the upper Churchill River], the leading track to the Athapuscow country." This seemed to be the shortest route to the Athabasca region, which lies somewhat northwest of Churchill Factory and still farther northwest of York; and the headwaters of the Churchill River rise just to the south of this region. Of course the orders Colen issued ignored the fact that he was sending men into almost unknown country where the principal waterways might have fast rapids, waterfalls, and long, shallow stretches that would make it impossible for canoes laden with goods to progress with any reasonable speed and without exhausting their crews.

Thompson's instructions were to seek the "track" via Reindeer Lake, which seemed to be a south-east exit from the Athabasca country somehow used by Indians coming down the Churchill to the Bay. While doing this he was to discover a shortcut back to York without using the waterway of the Saskatchewan, for the Saskatchewan's entry into Lake Winnipeg is some 450 miles south of York Factory as the crow flies, imposing an enormous detour of almost 1000 miles for traders based there, who, unlike the crow, had to follow rivers' windings.

The search for a way to Lake Athabasca at its extreme

eastern end took far longer than Thompson anticipated. In 1792 he left York Factory and wintered on the headwaters of the Nelson River, just north of Lake Winnipeg; the following spring he ascended part way up the Churchill, which he discovered was more a chain of lakes than a river, but he was unable to find Indian guides to lead him to Reindeer Lake and he returned to York. Perhaps his disappointment at not being able to make a good start towards Athabasca was softened by a letter from headquarters in London granting him the bonus given all servants who worked inland and also a reward "for your assiduity" — a brass compass, a fahrenheit thermometer, and a case of survey instruments. After collecting a fresh supply of trade goods, Thompson found his orders changed and he spent the fall drumming up trade on the north and south branches of the Saskatchewan.

Neither in 1794 nor 1795 did Thompson get much closer up "the leading track". He was working at the western end of what HBC men called the "Musk Rat" country — a rock-strewn, heavily-forested, water-logged region up to 400 miles wide that lay to the southwest of York between the Churchill and Nelson Rivers. The necessity of getting hunting supplies to the Indians before the Nor'Westers did and his inability to find any Indians who knew of an eastern route into Athabasca denied him time and opportunity to explore a way to and beyond Reindeer Lake. And in the winter of 1795-6 he was greatly irritated to find himself competing for furs with Nor'Westers and also with HBC men from Churchill Factory.

Finally in June 1796 he left Fairford House (at the junction of the Reindeer and Churchill Rivers) with two Chipewyan canoemen. He managed to make a quick exploration north past Reindeer Lake, over another lake (Wollaston), and then over a river (the Black) and yet another body of water

(Black Lake) to the eastern end of Lake Athabasca. In the course of this expedition he twice nearly lost his life.

The first time was while he was returning up Black River. Thompson's journal entry for the day in question records that

*. . . we came to one of the falls with a strong rapid both above and below it . . . they [the guides] were to track the canoe up by a line, walking on shore, while I steered it . . . the canoe took a sheer across the current . . . I sprang to the bow of the canoe, took out my clasp knife [and] cut the line . . . by this time I was on the head of the fall. All I could do was to place the canoe to go down bow foremost. In an instant the canoe was precipitated down the fall (twelve feet) and buried under the waves. I was struck out of the canoe and when I arose among the waves the canoe came on me and buried [me] beneath it . . .*

Thompson managed to swim ashore, but the stones of the river bottom had torn loose the flesh of his left foot from the heel almost to the toes. He had suffered many bruises from being flung against the rocks of the rapids, most of his clothing had been ripped off, and, worst of all, what provisions there were, the powder, ammunition, and fishing net had all been carried away and could not be found. (By some lucky chance the Indians were able to recover the cork-lined box containing his surveying instruments.) Thompson bound up his foot with some tent cloth, his men repaired the canoe with spruce gum and birchbark, and the trio set off again, hoping to catch fish and find wild berries to sustain them on the long return journey.

The next day Thompson, recognizing a few landmarks on the river's banks, remembered spotting an eagle's nest in a birch tree somewhere in the vicinity on the downstream voyage. He found the nest, and, as he had hoped, there were two young eagles in it. They put up a fierce struggle before being killed, and Thompson remarks that one of the Chipewyans

*incautiously laid hold of one of them, who immediately stuck the claws of one foot deep into his arm above the wrist. So firm were the claws in his arm, I had to cut off the leg at the first joint above the claws. Even then when we took out a claw it closed in again and we had to put bits of wood under each claw until we got the whole out.*

That evening, on cutting open the eagles, they found masses of yellow fat as well as flesh. One of the canoemen roasted and ate his ration of flesh and oiled himself with his portion of fat, but either forgot or neglected to advise his companions to eat only the flesh of fish-eating birds. They ate their pieces of fat and kept their meat as rations for the next day. That night the two men were awakened by agonizing attacks of dysentery, and these recurred during the next few days. What with only berries for food, the cool days and cold nights, and the dysentery that plagued him, Thompson became so weak that he felt it was useless to go any farther and he resigned himself to death. At this point the desperately sick men were lucky enough to meet some Chipewyans, who gave them broth to cure the dysentery and loaned Thompson provisions, flints, powder, and ammunition. They managed to complete the return voyage to Fairford House.

Late in August of that year Malcolm or Malchom Ross, Thompson's senior, arrived back from York with four small canoes of trade goods. In the course of discussion with Thompson about how to find a way into the fur-rich Atha-

basca country, Ross was somehow persuaded to accept the
Reindeer-Wollaston-Black route, despite his own preference
to go there by way of the upper Churchill and the Methye
Portage as he had done when accompanying Philip Turnor to
Lake Athabasca in 1790. Just why Thompson insisted on
recommending this route is something of a puzzle because he
had noted that, at the north end of Lake Reindeer, "we
proceeded up the Rivulet which we found shoal [shallow],
with many rapids, and soon led us to ponds and brooks, with
several carrying places, which connected them together for
fifty miles . . ." A fifty-mile portage would never be considered economic or practicable by any fur trader. Hudson's Bay
Company records suggest that Thompson may have deceived
himself into thinking it would be a good route because it was
reported that he wanted to return to Black Lake to complete
some observations for his surveying. At any rate, according to
Ross, Thompson said that he had made the trip in six weeks
out and back, and to Ross the route must have sounded
attractively short. He agreed to try it.

Although Thompson does not actually say so in his records
or in the *Narrative*, the expedition was a failure. After twelve
days the two men came to a creek beyond Reindeer Lake
that, according to Ross, Thompson admitted would not even
float "a small canoe with nothing in it but 3 blankets". They
found themselves late in the season in an area singularly
lacking in game, yet they and their party of seventeen had to
be fed through the winter. There was nothing to do but try
to survive where they were. Beside the lake they built a log
shack and, since it was the habit of the trade to give grand
titles to such crude structures, they called it Bedford House.
Then all of them settled down to the monotonous but vital
winter activity in which many an HBC fur trader was forced

to engage: finding enough fish and game to stay alive until
spring. To make matters worse, as Thompson's journal entries
of temperature readings confirm, it was one of the coldest
winters ever known in western North America.

On May 23rd, 1797, after several months of near starvation and the poorest of fur returns, Thompson began a
seventy-five mile walk to Fraser House, the nearest North
West Company post. In the course of the winter he had
decided to change employers.

# 3

# The Western Plains

The reasons why Thompson left the Hudson's Bay Company and joined the North West Company are not at all clear and probably never will be. His *Narrative* may be deliberately misleading when it says that he received a letter from Colen refusing to sanction further survey work, for no such letter has ever been found in Hudson's Bay archives or elsewhere: as the HBC correspondence for this period is still extant, it is odd that this one letter should be missing. The only other known source of information, a journal kept by Malcolm Ross, simply records that ". . . Mr. David Thompson acquainted Me with his time being out with your Honours and thought himself a free-born subject and at liberty to choose any service and enter the Canadian company's Employ".

It is true that Thompson's second three-year contract, made in 1794 (at £60 per annum), had terminated, but he was not free to walk away from the Company. It was normal practice for an HBC man to give his employers a year's notice of his intention to leave; without such notice the Company would be unable to arrange replacements and would suffer in its operations because at this time only one ship sailed to and from York carrying orders from London and taking back reports. Thompson must have known about this procedure. Furthermore Ross had intimated in writing his intention to

retire in 1797 and had received official notice via York in
September 1796 confirming his retirement and appointing
David Thompson to take charge upon Ross's relinquishing his
post of "Master to the Northward". It is unlikely that Ross
did not mention his coming retirement to Thompson; in any
case it is strange that Thompson nowhere mentions a promotion of which he would have to be informed and for which he
would have to be prepared. Was he afraid of the responsibil-
ity of managing the northwest thrust of the Company's
efforts? Was he uninterested in this prospect because he was
tired of trading at the expense of time that he would have
preferred to spend surveying? Or did he feel that he had
made a complete fool of himself in Company eyes in the
attempt to use the Reindeer Lake approach to Athabasca?

In changing his allegiance Thompson may have been influ-
enced by matters as simple as food and the time and energy a
Company man had to employ in keeping several steps ahead
of hunger. The Company had never imported much in the
way of food supplies. The men were expected to provide
their own; those working inland were often engaged in fishing
and hunting even while on the march. By comparison, the
Nor'Westers were nearly always well supplied with provisions,
the principal one being pemmican,* a plains-Indian invention.
For that matter Thompson's rivals were also better paid and

* According to Thompson: . . . *it is made of the lean and fleshy parts of the bison
[buffalo] dried, smoked, and pounded fine; in this state it is called beat meat; the
fat of the bison is of two qualities, called hard and soft; the former is from the
inside of the animal, which when melted is called hard fat (properly grease); the
latter is made from the large flakes of fat that lie on each side of the back bone,
covering the ribs, and which is readily separated and when carefully melted
resembles butter in softness and sweetness. Pemmican is made up in bags of
ninety pounds weight, made of the parchment hide of the bison with the hair on;
the proportion is twenty pounds of soft and the same of hard fat, slowly melted
together, and at a low warmth poured on fifty pounds of beat meat, well mixed
together . . . On the great plains there is a shrub bearing a very sweet berry of a*

better looked after by their employers. A Hudson's Bay
servant, leader though he might be, was expected to do his
own paddling, and at the end of a day of such labour would
eat whatever game or fish there was to eat and then roll
himself up in a blanket under a tree for the night. But Philip
Turnor reported a different state of affairs when informing
London about how a Nor'Wester travelled:

*. . . your Honours need never be surprised should you find
great difficulty in keeping your inland officers, as the Canadians prefer them to most others . . . It is not to be wondered
at that they should make your servants great offers, which is
constantly the case, when they give men which never saw an
Indian one hundred pounds PR. ANNUM, his feather bed
carried in the canoe, his tent, which is exceeding good,
pitched for him, his bed made, and he and his girl carried in
and out of the canoe; and when in the canoe he never
touches a paddle unless for his own pleasure. All of these
indulgences I have been an eyewitness to.*

These could all be reasons for Thompson's departure from
the Company. But there is one concrete piece of evidence
that could not help but influence him. It is likely that
Thompson was seriously disturbed by a letter of instruction

dark blue colour, much sought after. Great quantities are dried by the natives; in
this state these berries are as sweet as the best currants, and as much as possible
mixed to make pemmican.

Pemmican was made from any meat, but by far the best was that of the buffalo
— dried, softened by beating, and then mixed with dried berries and buffalo fat. A
complete diet in itself, pemmican lasted for years and could be eaten raw or
cooked. Above all it was a richer footstuff than either fish or meat itself and never
dulled the appetite as each of these did. One of the first "instant" or concentrated
foods, pemmican allowed the Nor'Westers to travel farther and faster because it
freed them from their earlier need to spend time fishing and hunting for food
supplies.

he received late in the summer of 1796 from Colen at York suggesting that certain of the Company's men working on the Churchill River "should be allowed to go into the Athapes-cow country" if they got far enough up the Churchill to be close to the edge of that region; if the Churchill men were to push on beyond him, Thompson was ordered to surrender his trading goods and provisions to them and return to Cumber-land House; if neither circumstance came to pass, he might be allowed to try again the next year. Colen had pointed out in an earlier letter that the men working out of Churchill Factory were reported to have had some success in getting large watercraft up the Churchill River and that it was more profitable to the Company to receive more furs more quickly at Churchill than fewer pelts by canoe at York. Thompson must have wondered what kind of future there was for his services as both "Surveyor and Trader". In the first place he seemed to be subject to sudden changes of orders; secondly there appeared to be no clear-cut plan that combined explor-ing and trading activities. Perhaps his discouragement at having his surveying activities curtailed was the principal reason for his abrupt departure.

On June 7th, 1797, Thompson left Fraser House and journeyed east to Grand Portage, Lake Superior, making as usual a survey of his route. The central depot of the North West Company, Grand Portage was on the north shore of the lake towards its western end and stood on the edge of a small bay that formed a natural amphitheatre with high, rocky hills as a backdrop. One trader described it as "the Headquarters and General Rendezvous for all who trade in this part of the world", which was true enough, although it was little more than a rather large stockaded post. Inside were sixteen well-weathered buildings of cedar and white spruce: six storehouses, a few dwelling houses, sheds, a counting-house or paymaster's office, the great hall or mess hall in which a hundred men could eat at a time, a stone-walled, tin-roofed magazine, and the *cantine*, where each of the Company's canoemen received his *régale* (a special issue of a white loaf, half a pound of butter, and a gill of rum) and where all of them spent their wages on food and tobacco or squandered most of their money on liquor. Nearby was the jail — the *pot au beurre* or butter-tub, as the voyageurs called it — where rowdy or excessively drunken characters were put to cool off. Along the lakefront was a ragged line of birchbark wigwams and a few log huts belonging to independent traders. Flowing past Grand Portage and into Lake Superior was a small stream. On one side of it were the upturned canoes that sheltered the voyageurs from Montreal; on the other the canoemen from the north country had erected their well-weathered hide tents. From the post itself an old Indian trail wound uphill to the northwest over nine miles of rocky, wooded terrain to a point above an unnavigable section at the mouth of the Pigeon River. This was the largest and the most difficult carrying-place encountered by the French, which they named Grand Portage, sometimes called the Great Carry, the way to the height of land separating the two drainage systems of the St Lawrence and Hudson Bay.

The Nor'Westers chose wisely when they made Grand Portage the hub of their trading operations. Water from three-quarters of Canada spills out through three huge drainage basins with low rims: the Great Lakes-St Lawrence system, the Saskatchewan River-Lake Winnipeg-Nelson River-Hudson Bay complex, and the Mackenzie River and its tributaries. The Nor'Westers knew from their French predecessors and their own travels that the rims or heights of land separating these basins could be crossed with relative ease because there was no great elevation in height from Montreal to Grand Portage or from there to Fort Chipewyan: indeed of all the portages between these points, none was much above 1500 feet in height. They had also discovered that a chain of interlocking lakes and rivers offered access by canoe from Montreal to almost any point in the interior or the northwest reaches of the continent. These circumstances explain many a fur-trade route and why, once over the height of land about 100 miles beyond Grand Portage, the Nor'Westers fanned out through almost every region north and west of Lake Superior and even southward toward the headwaters of the Mississippi. From the northern end of the Great Carry (or from the western end of Lake Superior) they paddled and portaged their way to man about a hundred fur posts in what are now Manitoba, Saskatchewan, Alberta, and Northwest Territories, and Wisconsin, Minnesota, and North Dakota. With David Thompson's aid, the Nor'Westers were destined to extend their operations into what are today British Columbia, Montana, Idaho, and Washington.

When Thompson arrived in late July, Grand Portage was overrun with people: several hundred *mangeurs du lard*, "eaters of pork" (their daily food ration, along with corn meal), the voyageurs who brought up from Montreal the large *cânots du maitre* laden with trade goods; almost as many *hommes du nord,* men of the north, the élite of the voyageurs, who manned the smaller, swifter *cânots du nord* that were used on the relatively shallow waterways between Grand Portage and the interior posts; various Indian bands, notably the Chippewa; the *bourgeois* or wintering partners in charge of canoe "brigades"; *commis*, the clerks or apprentice bourgeois; interpreters; the guides who led the brigades; and of course the inevitable packs of Indian dogs, which barked, growled, and yelped as they ran freely here and there. Every June and July, Grand Portage seethed with activity as Montrealers and winterers exchanged cargoes of goods and pelts and then sped off in opposite directions to avoid being caught short of their destinations by the freeze-up of river and lake.

At this time of the year, Grand Portage resembled an antheap, from which stretched a long line of mangeurs du lard, duty-bound to haul at least six ninety-pound *pièces* or packs of goods up the stony, often muddy trail to the group of ramshackle warehouses called Fort Charlotte at the edge of the Pigeon River. This was the hardest of labours and was only partly eased by the old portaging technique of using a tumpline — a leather sling, broad in the centre and tapering towards each end, that passed around a voyageur's forehead and was tied to a pack on his back. (It was not uncommon to carry a second pack atop the first.) By leaning forward into the broad portion of the tumpline, the voyageur was able to take some of the weight off his back and shuffle or half run in a slightly bent position. We are told by one Nor'Wester that "This is a labour which cattle cannot conveniently perform in summer, as both horses and oxen were tried by the Company without success." The pork-eaters had only two thoughts to sustain them on the Great Carry as their strength was further sapped by the summer's heat and by mosquitoes and black flies. They had already carried these goods over the thirty-six portages between Montreal and Grand Portage, and for many of them this was the thirty-seventh and last carry. Also, each man who succeeded in taking eight packs over the trail received a bonus of a silver dollar. Some of them would unhappily be deputed to paddle and portage trade goods another 500 or so miles up the Pigeon River to Rainy Lake House, the turnaround point for the Athabasca brigades. Owing to the brief northern summer the ice of river and lake broke up late and froze early, and thus the supply route between Grand Portage and the farthest posts had to be kept as short as possible.

The *engagé*, the salaried voyageur of the fur-trading companies, was a member of an almost unbelievably hardy breed of men. For much of the five months of the year between break-up and freeze-up, he paddled from dawn to dusk, sometimes driving loaded canoes for as much as eighteen hours at a stretch. Travellers carried by them have recorded that, after twelve hours of paddling with only three or four stops of ten to fifteen minutes each, these men were able to continue because they were still "fresh". In addition, whether transporting goods or furs, they often had to "line" or haul their canoe upstream by means of shoulder harnesses attached to bow and stern and run along a river's edge, sometimes through deep silt or over rocks and fallen trees, or by wading breast-high through the water; and they had to portage everything around any unnavigable ridge, fall, or rapid. This usually meant that each voyageur had to haul at least half a dozen pieces alongside or around the particular river obstruction. It has been calculated that by the time a man had taken three loads of 180 pounds apiece over a portage, he would have walked almost five miles for every mile-long portage. (Sometimes the canoe could be pushed up a rapid by means of eight- or ten-foot poles shod with metal, or the crew could get past an obstruction by unloading half the cargo and force-paddling through to calmer waters.) The voyageur did all this on a daily diet of a quart of cornmeal mush and pork fat if he was manning a freight canoe out of

Montreal carrying up to four tons of goods, or on fish and game, or wild rice and pemmican if he was a member of a team transporting a ton and a half of trading items or pelts in the north country.

For all that their achievement was Herculean, none of these men was of heroic proportions. They are described by an American visitor who travelled some of the fur routes out of curiosity:

*I can liken them to nothing but their own ponies. They are short, thick-set, and active, and never tire. A Canadian if born to be a labourer deems himself to be very unfortunate if he should chance to grow over five feet five or six inches; and if he shall reach five feet ten or eleven it forever excludes him from the privilege of becoming a voyageur. There is no room for the legs of such people in these canoes. But if he shall stop growing at about five feet four inches and be gifted with a good voice and lungs that never tire, he is considered as having been born under a most favourable star.* [2]

The same writer described how his canoemen took their craft out of the water, mended a breach in it, reloaded, cooked breakfast, shaved, washed, ate, and re-embarked — all in *fifty-seven* minutes.

It was literally a stroke of fortune for the penny-pinching Scots who ran the North West Company that many a Canadien, brought up on the tradition and tall tales of *le pays d'en haut*, the high or upper country, preferred the gay comradeship and carefree way of life of his brother canoemen to the dull, often poverty-stricken routine of farming in the fields of the St Lawrence valley. Unlike his masters, the voyageur made a mere pittance. A gregarious fellow, he sustained himself with the company of his comrades — and the occasional Indian girl — and his desire to travel to as many places as the Company would send him. He loved "the forest and the white water, the shadow and the silence, the evening fire, the stories and the singing and a high heart". Without him the Montreal fur trade would have been impossible to sustain. And without his skills, strength, and experience, such Nor'-Westers as Alexander Mackenzie, Simon Fraser, and David Thompson would have found it even more difficult, perhaps impossible, to explore the Northwest and the Pacific slope.

Thompson joined the North West Company at a time when it had great need of his skills as a surveyor and a geographer. A few years earlier the English colonists in North America had fought and won their war of independence with Great Britain. One of the clauses of the peace treaty that was signed in 1783 described part of the border between British North America and the newly formed republic of the United States as a line running through the middle of the St Lawrence River and the Great Lakes up to the Pigeon River, then on to the northwest corner of the Lake of the Woods, and, in effect, west along the 49th parallel until it met the head-waters of the Mississippi River. (None of the persons engaged in making the treaty knew whether or not this boundary line went anywhere near the headwaters of the Mississippi, for at this time *nobody* knew. However, the British and American diplomats negotiating in France all hoped that it did.) This boundary disturbed the Nor'Westers because it placed Grand Portage six miles on the American side of the frontier, and the terms of Jay's Treaty in 1794 made it clear that, sooner or later, the Americans would take over the depot (or Rendezvous, as Grand Portage was sometimes called). Thompson sought employment with the Company at a time when the Nor'Westers were even more concerned about where the 49th parallel actually ran so that they would know how many of their western posts were on British or American soil. Which of them would have to be moved and which would have to be abandoned?

The Company's orders to Thompson, who had been appointed "Surveyor and Map Maker", were quite explicit: he was instructed to survey the 49th parallel of latitude and find out where it ran, and it was his special duty to determine the exact position of the Company posts he visited in relation to the 49th parallel; if possible he was to extend his survey work to the upper Missouri River country and report on the Indians who lived there and were said to practise agriculture; and in the interests of science and history he was to look for the fossils of large animals.

On August 9th, 1797 Thompson and his party followed the usual trade route to the pays d'en haut by paddling up the Pigeon River, over Rainy Lake and the Lake of the Woods to the Winnipeg River and down its turbulent waters to the shores of "Lake Winnipeg (or the Sea) so called by the natives from its size". From its shallow, wind-tossed waters he swung westward along the Dauphin River to Lake "Manito" (Manitoba) and then north over this body of water to Lake "Winepegoos" (Winnipegosis). After veering southwest over Swan Lake and up the Swan River, Thompson and a companion, Cuthbert Grant, procured horses and continued southwest over the grassy prairies to the wooded valley of the Qu'Appelle River, a tributary of the Assiniboine, and then farther south still to the parklands along the Souris, another tributary, which occupied much the same latitude as Grand Portage. While making this long semi-circular sweep to the west, Thompson surveyed his route and, in the course of several side trips, visited and fixed the position of Company posts in much of the region bounded by his main travel route. (His calculations told him that he was still north of the 49th parallel.) In doing this he filled in many of the gaps between his former surveys of the Saskatchewan River country and the international boundary.

Late in November Thompson was at McDonnell's House, a Company post about a mile and a half from the entry of the Souris into the Assiniboine. From this post a well-beaten trade track wound south and then southwest across about 200 miles of prairie to the upper waters of the Missouri River where the Mandans lived, the "ancient agricultural Natives" Thompson had been asked to visit and report upon. The fact that winter had set in, a season when travelling on the open plains was both very difficult and exceedingly dangerous, made no difference to Thompson. He was determined to continue his explorations and rode off down the track accompanied by

*our guide and interpreter... a M. René Jussomme, who fluently spoke the Mandan language; Mr. Hugh McCrachan, a good-hearted Irishman who had been often to the [Mandan] villages and resided there for weeks and months; and seven French Canadians — a fine, hardy, good-humoured set of men, fond of full feeding, willing to hunt for it, but more willing to enjoy it . . .*

The first night out Thompson noted in his journal that the 8 p.m. temperature was 20 degrees below zero. At 7 a.m. the next morning it was -27°, and, there being a westerly breeze, "the men thought it too cold to proceed." On November 30th the temperature was -32° and four degrees colder still by 9 p.m. On the first day of December a gale came howling and screaming out of the southwest, and it was December 3rd

before they were able to continue. Luckily they had brought
along sled dogs and were spared the brute labour of hauling
their goods, tents, and provisions through the high drifts of
snow that cut visibility to about a quarter of a mile. More
snow-laden gales swept down on them in the next few days,
and the ten men had to be careful to walk in single file, at
times calling out to each other to ensure that no one had
wandered away into what has been called "the white death".
Even so, Thompson nearly lost a man on December 10th:

*. . . a gentle south wind arose and kept increasing. By 10
a.m. it was a heavy gale, with high drifts and dark weather —
so much so that I had to keep the compass in my hand . . .
By noon it was a perfect storm . . . Night came on. I could no
longer see the compass and had to trust to the wind. The
weather became mild with small rain but the storm continued
with darkness. Some of the foremost called to lie down
where we were, but as it was evident we were ascending a
gentle rising ground we continued and soon, thank good
Providence, my face struck against some oak saplings and I
passed the word that we were in the woods. A fire was
quickly made . . . but one man and a sled with the dogs were
missing. To search for the latter was useless; but how to find
the former we were at a loss and remained so for another half
an hour, when we thought we heard his voice. The storm was
still raging; we extended ourselves within call of each other.
The most distant man heard him plainly, went to him, raised
him up, and with assistance brought him to the fire, and we
all thanked the Almighty for our preservation.*

For the rest of that month the men staggered on over the frozen
prairie, somehow always being lucky enough to find an
occasional buffalo to kill. One day Thompson chased and shot

a bull from horseback in true plains-Indian style.

Thompson had been warned that the latter part of his route lay through Sioux territory. On the afternoon of December 24th, Thompson ordered his men to lie down in the snow when he spotted through his telescope a number of mounted Indians riding by some distance to the south; he later learned that this was a Sioux war party on the lookout for whatever unwary travellers they could plunder or take hostage. Six days later the weary group reached the safety and comfort of the Mandan villages strung out for several miles along the banks of the Missouri. They had taken thirty-two days to perform a journey that normally took only ten. But they had survived, and despite the terrible weather Thompson had worked out in the course of the journey the latitude of six different places and the longitude of three.

The indefatigable surveyor spent over a month with the peaceable Mandans. He used this time to good purpose, filling his journals with notes of the number of dwellings per village; the architectural details and the contents of these domed, sodded houses; the agricultural products of the people — maize, pumpkins, beans, and melons; the clean, neat appearance of his hosts and their homes; and about 400 words of their language. He was enchanted by the Mandans, describing them as "of a stature fully equal to Europeans . . . well limbed, the features good, the countenance mild and intelligent". At the same time he observed sternly that the famed Mandan dancing women, decorous and restrained though they were while stepping out to the music of drum, tambour, rattle, and a sort of flute,

*. . . were all courtesans, a set of handsome, tempting women . . . The Mandans have many ceremonies in all of*

*which the women bear a part, but my interpreter treated
them with contempt, which perhaps they merited.*

*The curse of the Mandans is an almost total want of
chastity. This the men with me knew, and I found it was
almost their sole motive for their journey hereto: the goods
they brought they sold at 50 to 60 per cent above what they
cost; and reserving enough to pay their debts and buy some
corn, [they] spent the rest on women.*

Thompson was fair enough to say later that the white men
who had visited the villages earlier had themselves not been
outstanding examples of chastity, adding that in his opinion
the Mandan morality was not so much given to matters of
desire and passion as it was to the avoidance, wherever
possible, of the crimes of theft, treachery, and murder.

Undaunted by the perils and pains of his December trek,
Thompson set out in January 1798 on the return journey,
the dog sleds loaded with wolf and fox furs and corn meal
and his men grumbling and stumbling along behind him. The
weather was almost as stormy throughout, and they took
twenty-four days.

Thompson stayed at McDonnell's House for three weeks,
checking over the astronomical observations he had made to
and from the Missouri and making a map of this survey. Then
he was off again, this time with three French Canadians, an
Indian guide, and three dog sleds heaped with provisions and
baggage.

Trudging along on snowshoes, Thompson traced the course
of the Assiniboine River east to where it joins the Red River,
the site of modern Winnipeg. Then he swung south and
marched up the broad, frozen Red, which is so winding a
river that Thompson remarks "An Indian compared the dev-

ious course of the river to a spy, who went here and there and everywhere to see what was going on in the country." On March 14th he arrived at a Company post at the mouth of the Pembina River and found it to be located at "48° 58' 24" north longitude". He was just south of the 49th parallel and was no longer on British soil.

Thompson rested for a week at the Pembina trading house and several times advised the manager, Charles Chaboillez, to move his post a few miles north. Then he marched on south over the Red (discovering a Company post at the mouth of another tributary), turned east up Red Lake River, and found another post (Cadotte's House) when he came to one of its tributaries, the Clearwater River. He noted that all these waterways flowed west and north.

All this time the physical going was becoming more and more exhausting because the first rains of spring were turning the snow to mush, and the weary travellers were soaked to the skin almost daily and had little opportunity to dry themselves when they encamped. Thompson actually had to return to Cadotte's House and stay for two weeks (during which time he enjoyed the company of its manager, Baptiste Cadotte, a Métis,* and his "very handsome" Métis wife) until the river ice broke up because "the snow thawing made the open country like a lake of open water". Determined to find the height of land that separates waters flowing north and south and near which would be the source of the Mississippi, he made a fresh start eastward from Cadotte's post on

*The great majority of "halfbreeds", as they were called, were born of the marriages or temporary liaisons between fur traders and Indian women. Those whose fathers were French or French Canadian, and therefore of the Roman Catholic faith, were known as Métis or *bois-brûlés*. Many of them farmed in the Red River country and supplied produce to the fur trade. Ultimately many Metis joined the hunt for buffalo in order to supply pemmican to the trade.

April 9th, this time by canoe. Stalled again by ice nine days later, he built a sled and put the canoe and his supplies on it. He and his four men (and the Indian wife of one of the men) harnessed themselves to the sled and they hauled it seventeen miles through rain and sleet until they came upon open water again (Lower Red Lake). On April 27th, after traversing a bewildering number of small lakes and brooks due south of Lower Red Lake, the party arrived at a lake (Turtle Lake) that has a waterway exiting to the southwest, and Thompson decided that this was the "source of the Mississippe". He was wrong by a matter of a few miles. A generation later it was decided that the source is Itasca Lake, a body of water just a little farther south and west. (Even this seems to be a matter for dispute. Some geographers today claim that the source is Little Elk Lake, a tiny body of water to the south of Turtle Lake). However, Thompson was at least 100 miles below the border and had exposed the error of the diplomats in supposing that the 49th parallel crossed the headwaters of the mighty Mississippi.

Thompson headed southeast for some distance and then cut across country to the westernmost end of Lake Superior, discovering three more posts on American soil in the course of this particular survey. He did not return right away to Grand Portage as he could have done with relative ease by following Superior's north shore for about 150 miles. His geographer's instinct sensed an opportunity to be utilized, and he made his way down to the south side of the lake and surveyed this shoreline of almost 700 miles all the way east to the falls of Sault Ste Marie, over which Superior waters pour on their way to Lakes Huron and Michigan. Here, on May 28th,

*I had the pleasure of meeting Sir Alexander Mackenzie, the*

*celebrated traveller who was the first to follow down the
great stream of water flowing northward from the Slave Lake
into the Arctic Sea, and which great river bears his
name . . . The next day the Honourable William McGillivray
arrived. These gentlemen were the agents and principal partners of the North West Company; they requested me to
continue the survey of the lake round the east and north
sides to the Grand Portage . . .*

Thompson arrived back at the Rendezvous on June 7th.
He had been gone ten months and had completed almost
4000 miles of surveying. Even Alexander Mackenzie, the
renowned explorer, was quite astounded and remarked that
Thompson had performed more in ten months than he expected could have been done in two years.

# 4

## The Western Mountains

In 1800, at the annual summer meeting at Grand Portage, the partners and agents of the North West Company voted to send an exploring expedition from the headwaters of the Saskatchewan through the Rocky Mountains to the Pacific. The impetus for this move was Thompson's discovery of where the forty-ninth parallel ran and, shortly afterwards, the loss of the southern and southwestern posts. However the reasons for looking far to the west were a little older in origin.

In 1741, twenty-nine years before David Thompson was born, the Danish navigator Vitus Bering sailed from Siberia to explore the coast of what is now Alaska for the Russian government. In the course of the voyage he and his men discovered a marine animal that possesses a wonderfully soft, glossy fur — the sea otter — and from then on it was hunted and killed as brutally and relentlessly as the beaver ever was on the North American mainland. The demand for the sea-otter's pelt, perhaps the finest and hardest-wearing of all furs, was to rise steadily, and there came a time when a single skin was sold in Canton, China, by American traders for $2000.

Thirty-five years after Bering's voyage, the great British navigator, Captain James Cook, made his third famous voyage of discovery, which lasted from 1776 to 1779. On his way up the coast of North America to find the Pacific gateway of the Northwest Passage, Cook entered an inlet he called King George's Sound (Nootka Sound) off the west coast of what he thought at first was the mainland and which was really Vancouver Island. Here he made such friendly contact with the Nootka Indians that a brisk trade in sea-otter garments and pelts quickly developed between these natives and his crew. Cook noted that the Indians greatly desired metal, preferably brass, and in the course of his two-month stay he learned that the trading system going on in the lee of his ship extended far eastward into the interior. He guessed that the source of the trade goods was the Hudson's Bay Company, Mexico, or "Canada". His third guess was right: they had come from the Pedlars.

Soon after Cook's report to the Admiralty was published in 1784, the Nor'Westers, especially Peter Pond, learned of the sea otter. Actually Pond, the pioneer and organizer of what came to be known as the Athabasca Department of the Company, heard the news ahead of many of his colleagues. By 1784, with information often acquired from Indians and voyageurs, Pond had worked out on paper, crudely but more or less correctly, many of the principal waterways of western North America, a version of which he presented to the Congress of the newly established United States in the course of a brief visit in 1785 to Washington. Upon his return to Quebec, Pond was informed of Cook's descriptions of the sea-otter trade. Thereafter he spent many an Athabasca night trying to work out the geographical problem of an overland route to the Pacific. (Pond was never able to cope with the mathematics of longitude; as a result he assumed that the Pacific was just a few days' canoeing west of Lake Athabasca.) After further questioning of Indian customers, he concentrated his attention on a distant body of water (Great

Slave Lake) out of which a river was said to run to the westward (which is what the Mackenzie initially does). Pond calculated that this river must be somewhere about 64° N, and, when he looked at his copy of Cook's text and maps, he saw just north of 60° N a sound called Cook's inlet (at the head of which is the modern Anchorage, Alaska), which the explorer reported had a great flow of fresh water at its eastern end. After much speculation, Pond decided that this must be where the river had its exit. But Pond was not destined to undertake the arduous search for "Cook's River". His successor in Athabasca, Alexander Mackenzie, was the one who tested Pond's theory of a navigable waterway to the Pacific.

Where Pond was primarily obsessed by a geographical problem, initially Mackenzie was much more concerned to find a waterway to the Pacific so that trade goods and furs could be freighted in bulk between Europe and the Northwest instead of being hauled in ninety-pound pieces across 3000 miles of wilderness from Montreal and back again. Long before most of his compatriots did, Mackenzie clearly saw that a cheap supply route by sea was the basic strength of the Hudson's Bay Company, together with the fact that the Bay depots were farther west than Grand Portage. Later, after further reflection, Mackenzie added to his original idea the notion of combatting Russian trading activities on the Pacific coast and of getting a share – if not all – of the rich sea-otter trade that was being built up in Chinese ports by individual American fur traders working up and down the Pacific coast. Being an unusually profit-minded Scot, he envisaged exchanging furs for trade goods on the Pacific coast and then selling these furs in China for much more money than they would fetch in Britain or Europe.

Mackenzie's efforts to find "Cook's River" took him in 1789 to the Arctic Ocean and then in 1793 over the boiling rapids, tumbling waters, and brutal portages of the Peace, Parsnip, (upper) Fraser, West Road, and Bella Coola Rivers. He reached the Pacific at Burke Channel. But where he had hoped to find a smooth-flowing river leading from Lake Athabasca, he had had to risk life and limb in the course of 900 miles of raging mountain waters that are still barely navigable today and for which birchbark canoes, laden close to the gunwales with furs or trade goods, would be totally unfitted.

Mackenzie resigned from the North West Company in 1799, but his vision of an overland route to the Pacific was shared by William McGillivray, now the chief superintendent of the Company, and in particular by his brother Duncan, who decided to find a way through the Rocky Mountains. Late in 1800 Duncan McGillivray and David Thompson made plans to begin the push to the Pacific by establishing trade on the far side of the mountains. They hoped to find a pass by way of the headwaters of the North or South Saskatchewan.

The Company's explorer and surveyor arrived at Rocky Mountain House on the North Saskatchewan River accompanied by a wife. On his way down to the Rendezvous from the Athabasca country in the June of 1799, Thompson stopped off for a while at the Nor'Wester post at Isle-à-la-Crosse, which at one time had been operated by Patrick Small, a wintering partner who had been in the pays d'en haut as early as 1779. Small had retired to England to become a prosperous London merchant, leaving behind his Indian wife, their son Patrick, and two daughters, Nancy and Charlotte. Charlotte was fourteen years old, an age at which Indian and Métis girls were often married, and Thompson

took her as his wife in the manner dictated by Indian custom
— that is, by courting her with the permission of several of
her male relatives and then declaring her to be his woman and
confirming their union by making several gifts to these kins-
men. His journal entry for June 10th contains the terse
comment "This day married Charlotte Small." There is no
description of Charlotte by her husband or by any other
contemporary. However, we do know that their marriage was
an enduring union. She went with him on many of his travels,
and it was no uncommon sight to see Thompson and his wife,
accompanied by several young children, in a canoe going up
or down the Saskatchewan or encamped in a deep mountain
valley. Charlotte bore him seven sons and six daughters.
Unlike many Nor'Westers, Thompson did not abandon his
halfbreed wife (or his family) when he left the western fur
country. They were only parted by his death fifty-eight years
after they married, and even then Charlotte only survived
him by three months.

Shortly after it emerges from the rugged foothills of the
Rocky Mountains the North Saskatchewan River ceases to
flow east and, where the Clearwater River joins it, takes a
sharp turn north. Here in 1799 John McDonald of Garth
built Rocky Mountain House for the Nor'Westers, and this
was where Duncan McGillivray and Thompson met in October 1800 to probe for passes through to the Pacific slope. By
way of preliminary survey, McGillivray reconnoitred (unsuc-
cessfully) to the northwest as far as the upper waters of the
Athabasca River. Thompson rode southwest through Piegan
territory and then turned due west into heavily forested
foothills; here he met a party of Kootenays looking for the
Nor'Westers' post. He led them there and traded with them
but learned little of the geography of their home on the other

side of the massive, saw-toothed barrier of the Rockies or how they had managed to make their way east. The best he could do was send back with these Indians two of his voyageurs in the hope that they would discover something about travel routes and fur trapping in the mountains. (There is no record that these men returned.)

In the course of the winter McGillivray was crippled by rheumatism, so much so that the following summer he was forced to return to Grand Portage on crutches. Before he left he deputed James Hughes, a Company partner, "to penetrate to the Pacific Ocean". Thompson accompanied Hughes' party as surveyor, but records that their Indian guide led them up a minor river valley "to steep rocks and we had to return, and I passed the summer at the House . . . Thus ended the business [of exploring] of 1801."

After this failure, except for ordering Simon Fraser to establish fur posts in the interior of what is now central British Columbia, the Company ignored the Pacific slope for several years. The gradual trapping out of beaver was making the competition for furs ever keener, and the Nor'Westers now found HBC men not far behind them or in some cases at posts alongside them. As a result, Thompson had to return to many familiar areas as a trader, first to the Athabasca country, where the Hudson's Bay Company had at long last established a post, then to his old stamping ground, the Musk Rat country southwest of Hudson Bay. He solaced himself during these years (1802-6) by taking many astronomical observations and utilizing his earlier calculations and notes as he gradually outlined his map of the western fur country, a labour he had begun in 1799.

A further solace to Thompson must have been his promotion beyond the official rank of clerk. When he was summoned to the Rendezvous in 1804, Grand Portage had been abandoned and had been replaced by a new depot forty-five miles farther east along the north shore of Lake Superior at the mouth of the Kaministiquia River (in the vicinity of Thunder Bay, Ont.); here an old French route linked Lake Superior with the Rainy River-Lake of the Woods route to the pays d'en haut. The Company's new, larger Rendezvous, which came to be called Fort William in honour of William McGillivray, was in effect a company town. On the deep protected shore of the Kaministiquia a sizeable dock sheltered the high-prowed cânots du maître and a growing fleet of lake ships. In the centre of the depot was a large building that contained two private rooms for the use of the principal agents when in residence and a huge banqueting hall, which was described many years later by a visitor:

*The dining-hall is a noble apartment, and sufficiently capacious to entertain two hundred. A finely executed bust of the late Simon M'Tavish [the organizer of the Company] is placed in it, with portraits of various proprietors . . . At the upper end of the hall there is a very large map of the Indian country, drawn with great accuracy by Mr. David Thompson, Astronomer to the Company, and comprising all their trading-posts, from Hudson Bay to the Pacific Ocean and from Lake Superior to Athabasca and Great Slave Lake.*[3]

It was in this hall in July 1804 that Thompson was declared a partner in the "concern" — in modern terms, a member of the board of directors.

In June 1806 Thompson left his post in the Musk Rat country never to return to it. That year, at the annual meeting of the partners and agents at Fort William, John McDonald of Garth, the Nor'Wester in charge of the Fort des

Prairies [Saskatchewan] Department, had Thompson transferred to his command because he wanted him to find a way through the western mountains and to establish trading posts on the Pacific slope. The course of the fur trade on the North Saskatchewan was, as usual, from one exploited beaver region to the next untapped one westward, and McDonald was eager to move into the mountains, the next likely source of profits.

McDonald knew Thompson well; they were actually brothers-in-law, McDonald having married Nancy Small. He considered Thompson a good trader, a fearless traveller, and a man who was liked and respected by Indians. Indeed, McDonald's few criticisms of his brother-in-law had to do with his piety, his passion for surveying, and his total unwillingness to drink or to employ liquor when dealing with customers. Thompson had seen so many Indian men and women debased or made murderous by spirits that he had acquired a violent aversion to its use as a trading bribe. The following passage from his *Narrative* shows how strongly he felt:

*I was obliged to take two kegs of alcohol, overruled by my partners (Messrs Donald McTavish and John McDonald of Garth), for I had made it a law to myself that no alcohol should pass the mountains in my company, and thus be clear of the sad sight of drunkenness and its many evils. But these gentlemen insisted upon alcohol being the most profitable article that could be taken for the Indian trade ... When we came to the defiles of the mountains I placed the two kegs of alcohol on a vicious horse, and by noon the kegs were empty and in pieces ... I wrote to my partners what I had done and that I would do the same to every keg of alcohol, and for the next six years I had charge of the fur trade on the west side*

*of the mountains, no further attempt was made to introduce
spirituous liquors.*

Thompson knew perfectly well that taking goods into the
mountains, particularly guns and ammunition, would not be
easy while Piegans kept intermittent watch on Rocky Mountain House. Over the course of many years, they had used
guns bought from the Hudson's Bay Company and the Nor'-
Westers to drive several plains Indian groups into the mountains and had no desire to see a balance of power develop as
soon as their enemies in turn acquired firearms. Nor did they
wish to lose their own lucrative trade in European goods with
these tribes. Nonetheless, he made preparations for an attempt to cross over to the Pacific slope in 1807; late in 1806
Thompson ordered one of his men, "Jaco" Finlay, a halfbreed guide and interpreter, to follow the North Saskatchewan into the mountains in the hope that he could blaze a
trail through on his own or with the aid of the Kootenays.

As it happened, fate lent a helping hand at this particular
time. In the summer of 1806 part of the famous Lewis and
Clark expedition overland to the Pacific had been attacked
by some Piegans, and two warriors had been killed; after
brooding on the incident all winter, several war parties raged
south to the upper Missouri in the early summer of 1807 to
avenge those deaths on anyone who crossed their paths. The
way to the mountains was open.

On May 10th Thompson and his party, which included his
wife and their three children, the youngest on his mother's
back, toiled up the banks of the North Saskatchewan to the
Kootenay Plains, a beautiful, broad stretch of grass and
woodland where the Kootenay were accustomed to camp on
their journeys to and from the plains to hunt buffalo and

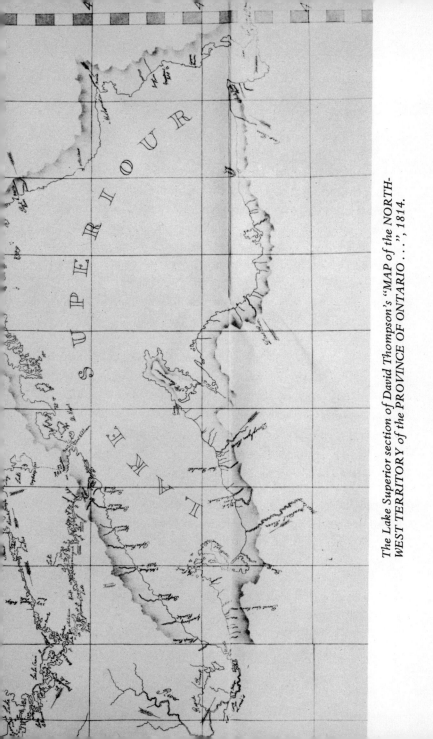

*The Lake Superior section of David Thompson's "MAP of the NORTH-WEST TERRITORY of the PROVINCE OF ONTARIO . . .", 1814.*

where Finlay seems to have maintained an advance post of Rocky Mountain House. On the next stage west they had to lead pack horses into the mountains through the entrance dominated on the north by the crags of Mt Wilson and on the south by the massive ledges of Mt Murchison. (At this point, Thompson was roughly halfway between the modern towns of Banff and Jasper.) Once through this opening they followed Finlay's badly blazed trail up a pleasantly wooded valley containing a broad, placid river (the Howse) until they were in an open, park-like area at the foot of a gap in the mountains. Barely fifty miles north was the cluster of mighty peaks that cradles the greatest body of ice in the Rocky Mountains — the 130-square-mile Columbia Icefield, a relic of the ice ages and the genesis of many glaciers.

*Here among the stupendous and solitary wilds covered with eternal snow, and mountain connected with mountain by immense glaciers, the collection of ages and on which the beams of the sun make hardly any impression when aided by the most favourable weather, I stayed fourteen days more, impatiently waiting for the melting of the snows of the height of land.*

The height of land is the continental divide that twists and winds its way through the Rocky Mountains and separates waters flowing to the Arctic, to Hudson Bay, and to the Pacific. Where the divide crosses the top of the Howse valley is what Thompson called "Mountain Portage", a narrow wilderness trail (Howse Pass) leading to the western side of the mountains.

On June 25th the little party made the stiff climb up to the divide, which is 5000 ft above sea level here and flanked on the west by the awesome, glistening masses of the Fresh-field Icefield. It took them five days to descend the western slope, days spent carefully guiding tired, bad-tempered pack horses alongside a raging torrent (Blaeberry River) that tumbles down through some 40 miles of heavily timbered country before finally levelling out on the broad floor of a huge valley. The Blaeberry enters a larger waterway that Thompson christened the "Kootenae". (At this point he was just a few miles north of Golden, British Columbia.) Deceived both by the waterway's northward flow and its location so far from the Pacific coast — and thus completely unaware that it was the upper Columbia — Thompson turned south and made his way about 70 miles to a point close to a mountain lake (Windermere, the lower of the two lakes from which the Columbia flows), where he had his men build Kootenae House.

Anticipating trouble from the Piegans, Thompson made sure that the post was stockaded on three sides, the fourth side being the steep bank of the river. Perhaps it was as well that he did fortify his trading centre because a war party came late in the fall, apparently not so much to attack as to hang about and disrupt any trading with the Kootenays.

*I had six men with me and ten guns, well loaded. The house was perforated with large augur holes, as well as the bastions. Thus they [the Piegans] remained for three weeks without daring to attack us. We had a small stock of dried provisions, which we made go as far as possible. They thought to make us suffer for want of water, as the bank we were on was 20 feet high and very steep, but at night by a strong cord we quietly and gently let down two brass kettles, each holding four gallons, and drew them up full.*

The Piegans tired of their watch and withdrew, leaving Thompson free to spend the winter doing a lot of profitable business with his new customers.

Thompson's intense concentration on business matters for the next two years was not a little due to his being a partner and therefore a profit-sharer in the Company. Also, McDonald of Garth left the Northwest in 1808 owing to ill health, and the district west of the mountains was formed into the Columbia Department with Thompson in charge. His growing family provided another motive for his near-exclusive attention to business, as is revealed in a letter he sent to Alexander Fraser, a fellow Nor'Wester. It is dated "21 Dec. 1810, Athabaska River, foot of the Mountains":

*. . . It is my wish to give all my children an equal and good education; my conscience obliges me to it and it is for this I am now working in this country . . . If all goes well and it pleases good Providence to take care of me, I hope to see you and a civilized world in the autumn of 1812.*

Thompson had been due to "go down in rotation" to Montreal for twelve-months' leave in 1808, yet there was no respite for him that year. He was only thirty-eight years old, but like many colleagues of his age he was discovering that the rigours of the fur trade were better suited to younger men and he wanted to acquire as much money as possible and retire. He also had a long-cherished ambition to produce a map of the western country. Thompson needed only a little more time west of the mountains to complete the geographical information he had already gathered on his own, from Mackenzie's report of his voyage to the Pacific, and also from notes being sent him by an old friend and fellow partner,

Simon Fraser, who was trading farther north in the Company's New Caledonia Department and was at this time seeking the elusive Columbia.

Between April and December 1808 Thompson accomplished a fantastic amount of travel, in the course of which he opened up several new trading areas. First of all he and a few of his men set off south down that extraordinary valley we call the Rocky Mountain Trench, an immense trough anywhere from two to ten miles wide that separates the Canadian Rockies from the other western ranges. After one day's canoeing from Kootenae House, they portaged a few miles to the source of what Thompson called the "Flat Bow" or "McGillivray's river" (really the Kootenay, a tributary of the Columbia), which carried them far down the Trench and, in the course of a great bending turn back to the north, into the northwest of present-day Montana and Idaho, where they came upon a camp of Kootenays and Flatheads just west of the Montana-Idaho border. After extracting a promise from these Indians to trade with him, which may not have been difficult because they had been attacked with firearms by Piegans a few days earlier, Thompson pushed on briefly downriver to Kootenay Lake (in southeast British Columbia). Returning upriver to the Indians' camp, he bought horses for his party and set off northeast across country until he met up with the Kootenay again, which led him back to Kootenae House. He had been gone six weeks and had journeyed about 600 miles.

A few days later, loading his family and the winter's take in furs onto horses, he led his party back over the pass above the headwaters of the North Saskatchewan and embarked in a canoe they had left at Kootenay Plains the previous year. Before travelling to Rainy Lake House some 1500 miles to the east, he left his family at a post some way downriver from Rocky Mountain House — his wife was within a month or two of giving birth to their fourth child. On August 2nd he reached the Rainy Lake supply point and hurriedly replaced his bales of furs with packs of trade goods. Two days later he was heading west, and by October 31st he and his family (including a new baby boy) were back on the Columbia. Before the year was out he dispatched his principal assistant, Finan McDonald, to build and occupy a trading post down at the big bend of the Kootenay (close to modern Libby, Montana).

In April 1809, when the winter's trade at Kootenae House was finished, Thompson took out the season's pelts as far as Fort Augustus on the site of the present city of Edmonton, arranged the transport of provisions and goods to his mountain base, and by August was back again at the western end of the big bend of the Kootenay (in the vicinity of Bonner's Ferry, Idaho). Again obtaining horses from Indian friends, he rode south to Pend Oreille Lake, where he found a large camp of Flatheads and other Indians. On the east side of the lake, close to the mouth of the Clark Fork River, he built Kullyspell House. Among other things, the presence of this post in the region meant that the Flatheads were able to

*RIGHT Each time Thompson journeyed south down the Rocky Mountain Trench, he had to cross the body of water (Columbia Lake, B.C.) that is the source of the Columbia River. The view here is from the lake's southern end. On the right are the western slopes of the Rocky Mountains. In the foreground can be seen the remains of a man-made channel that once linked the lake with streams leading to the upper waters of the Kootenay River. It is said that the men of Thompson's Columbia Department dug this water connection in order to avoid portaging goods and furs to and from the Kootenay.*

trade for guns. In 1810 they defeated a raiding party of Piegans, and Thompson offers a shrewd explanation of this victory.

*All those who could procure guns soon became good shots, which the Piegan Indians, their enemies . . . severely felt. For they are not good shots except a few; they are accustomed to fire at the bison on horseback within a few feet of the animal. It gives them no practice at long shots at small marks. On the contrary the Indians on the west side of the mountains are accustomed to fire at the small antelopes at a distance of one hundred and twenty yards, which is a great advantage in battle where everyone marks out his man.*

In November he followed the Clark Fork upstream, built a second post for the Flathead trade called Saleesh (Salish) House, and wintered there.

While working assiduously to increase the Company's trade during these years, Thompson did not entirely resist the temptation to do some surveying over and above what was possible in the course of his business trips. Thus he tracked what he called the "Kootenae" to its source in a mountain lake (Columbia) in Windermere valley, still unaware that it was the Columbia. While based at Kullyspell House several hundred miles south of this valley, he twice canoed westward over Pend Oreille Lake and down the turbulent Pend Oreille River to find out if it could be used as a trade route. But its waters proved to be unnavigable, both in the fall of 1809 and in the spring of 1810, and he gave up the search. Had he portaged or marched another thirty miles on the second occasion he would have come to a large waterway flowing southwest, and it would have taken him down to the Pacific

Ocean. It was the great river of the Pacific Northwest that first, Alexander Mackenzie, and then Simon Fraser had tried but failed to find: the Columbia.

# 5

## The Columbia

In mid-April 1810 Thompson left Finan McDonald in charge at Salish House and set out with numerous pack loads of furs on the long haul to Rainy Lake House far to the east. He and his party managed to reach the Blaeberry River without incident, although on his way up the Rocky Mountain Trench he noted on June 9th:

*... we saw the fresh tracks of Piegan scouts ... On examining the tracks [we] found they had gone up the river to recross the mountains. Had we been a few hours sooner we should have had to fight a battle, which thank God is thus avoided.*

Thompson was doubtless relieved that he had left his wife and family at a post on the Saskatchewan the previous year. He left them at Winnipeg House, close to Lake Winnipeg, in 1810 and was to be very grateful that he had done so.

Once up and over the continental divide, he embarked on the clear, ice-cold waters of the Howse River, deep in the alpine valley fed by the glaciers of the Freshfield Icefield. As always at this time of year the meltwater from ice and snow made the upper waters of the river a raging torrent. A careful watch had to be kept for sawyers — trees torn from the banks by the current and later grounded by their roots in shallow river stretches just near enough to the surface to rip a birchbark canoe to shreds and leave its occupants at the mercy of rock and rapid. Natural hazards were not the only worries Thompson had. On June 20th he records making camp at the foot of high crags of limestone in case he was attacked by Piegans. He had good reason to be wary because Indians were often unpredictable in the way they expressed their anger. The history of the fur trade includes a few incidents where the enmity of Indians cost a trader his life when he might well have anticipated only being looted of his goods. As Thompson remarks of the Piegans, "they were determined to wreak their vengeance on the white men who crossed the mountains to the west side and furnished arms and ammunition to their enemies." In all probability they were out to kill him as a warning to the Company to confine its operations east of the mountains.

Thompson's progress downriver was swift. Within a few days he arrived at Fort Augustus. By July 4th he was at Cumberland House and a mere eighteen days later was several hundred miles east at Rainy Lake House.

It is at this point in Thompson's life that he becomes the subject of controversy and argument. There is still confusion about the orders that awaited him at Rainy Lake House. In the opinion of at least two Canadian historians, he was instructed to find and survey the Columbia to its mouth as quickly as possible and thus stake a territorial claim to the entire Columbia region before an American rival, John Jacob Astor's Pacific Fur Company, did so by establishing a trading post at the mouth of the river. This theory, based on the writings of several of Thompson's contemporaries, is convincing but for one thing: it lacks clear and conclusive proof that Thompson was ever given such instructions. The minutes of the annual meeting at Fort William that ended on July 18th, 1810, record among other things the continued assignment of David Thompson to the Columbia Department — that and nothing more. There is no mention whatever of a plan to outrace Astor to the estuary of the Columbia. (Duncan McGillivray, the principal Company advocate of pushing on to the Pacific, might have instigated a plan to outrace Astor, but he had died in 1808.) The partners and agents present at Fort William in 1810 were infinitely more interested in procuring greater quantities of furs from the Pacific slope, since by this time many parts of the Northwest were rapidly becoming trapped out. As a matter of fact, the costs of hauling goods and furs all the way to and from the slowly developing New Caledonia and Columbia Departments were cutting very heavily into profits; the partners and agents were therefore desperately anxious to open up new trading areas in the far west.

What does Thompson say about his orders for 1810-11? The *Narrative* contains the sole statement that "my object was to be at the Pacific Ocean before the month of August", presumably a reference to the fact that, after that date (in 1811), he would have trouble getting back to the mountains in time to cross over to pick up supplies before the winter set in. However, in volume 35 of David Thompson's journals, preserved today in the Ontario government's Department of Public Records and Archives, Toronto, there are six foolscap sheets in his handwriting entitled *Discoveries from the east side of the Rocky Mountains to the Pacific Ocean by David Thompson*. An entry under 1810 reads:

*April 15. Set off to recross the Mountains with the furs &c. to Lac la Pluie [Rainy Lake], where we arrived July*

*22nd, 1810. Mr. Astor, having engaged some of the clerks of
the N.W. Co'y, formed a company and sent a vessel around
Cape Horn to the Columbia. Everything was changed ... I
was now obliged to take 4 canoes and to proceed to the
mouth of the Columbia to oppose them. Accordingly I set
off from Lac la Pluie.*

This statement is not conclusive proof that he was told to
confront Astor's men: there is no confirmation of this in any
contemporary record. However, an order to go and *oppose*
the Astorians would be a typical and unexceptional Company
directive: meet competition head on and outsell it or under-
sell it. The Nor'Westers had done this for years with HBC
customers and with those of independent traders. What did it
matter if an American company got to the mouth of the
Columbia ahead of the North West Company? Territorial
claims had never bothered the Nor'Westers; for decades they
had been trading in regions that were, by act of Parliament,
the legal territory of the Hudson's Bay Company. In any case
the Nor'Westers were already established at various points on
the Pacific slope and could, if they ever wanted, put forward
a stronger claim of their own. Mackenzie had pioneered the
way in 1793. In 1805-8 Simon Fraser had supervised the
establishment of several fur posts in New Caledonia (central
British Columbia) and had followed the river that bears his
name down to the Pacific. (It was Thompson who named the
river after him.) And Thompson and the men of his Department had been trading for some years west of the continental
divide and also south of the 49th parallel.

What is much more baffling than the orders Thompson
received is his behaviour between late July and the end of
October 1810. The *Narrative* account of this period is barely

three pages long, though this time span contained some curious happenings. On his way back to the Columbia via the North Saskatchewan, Thompson was out of contact with his canoe brigade for quite some time, although the reasons for this are not made clear. He implies that blood was shed between his voyageurs and Piegans but fails to describe or explain what happened during this encounter. Strangely enough we get no help from Thompson's journal for the period because his entries cease on July 22nd and do not begin again until October 29th. Did he lose his journal and have to rely on his memory when he came to write the *Narrative* in the 1840s? Or did he, as some historians have implied, destroy it because it contained an account of actions of which he was ashamed? The Thompson journals in the Ontario archives are by no means complete for the years 1801 and 1802, and so the loss of an 1810 journal may have a perfectly natural explanation, not least because Thompson lugged his field notes up hill and down dale in the course of thousands of miles of travel.

At any rate according to the *Narrative* he travelled the latter part of the return journey across the plains on horseback in company with an assistant, William Henry, and two Indian hunters. In order to conserve supplies of pemmican in the canoes, they were seeking buffalo to kill and cache for the voyageurs. Thompson normally kept in touch with his brigade every three days and expected to meet up with his men, he says, on or about October 16th. When they did not appear, he sent Henry and one of the Indians in search of them, and they reported back with the information that

*they had seen a camp of Piegans on the bank of the river [the N. Saskatchewan], that a short distance below the camp they had descended the bank to the river side and found where the canoes had been. They [the canoemen] had made a low rampart of stones to defend themselves and there was blood on the stones; they [Henry and the Indians] went below this and fired a shot in hopes of an answer from the canoes, but it was not returned.*

Thompson then goes on:

*I told them that they had acted very foolishly, and that we must start at the dawn of the day and ride for our lives; on this we acted the next morning and rode off . . .*

Up to now he has used the first person singular in his *Narrative,* but at this point he mysteriously switches to the plural: "we found them [the men] at a trading post lately deserted," he writes, and adds that "after much consultations, we fully perceived that we had no further hopes of passing in safety by the defiles of the Saskatchewan River, and that we must now change our route to the defiles of the Athabaska River . . . which would place us in safety, but would be attended with great inconvenience, fatigue, suffering, and privation . . . " But who were the unexplained "we"? It would be natural to suppose that this referred to Thompson and his assistant, William Henry. Or was this Thompson's way of also referring to William's cousin, Alexander Henry, without actually mentioning his name?

Alexander Henry the Younger (so called to distinguish him from his uncle of the same name, a contemporary of the Frobishers and Peter Pond) was another North West Company partner. His journals tell a very different story of what happened at and near the "post lately deserted". Henry was travelling ahead of his own canoes to Rocky Mountain

House, which had ceased to be used as a fur post, but which he was going to revive as a trading centre. According to Henry, who was a witness to some of the incidents involving Thompson and his brigade, the canoemen last saw their leader on September 15th — a month earlier than the date Thompson gives. Henry relates the canoemen's story that Black Bear, a friendly Piegan chief, met them and warned that "four tents of Piegans" were waiting upstream to prevent their going up to the headwaters of the North Saskatchewan. The brigade returned to Rocky Mountain House where Henry, who planned to winter there, came upon them on October 5th, unharmed and still awaiting the appearance of a leader they said they had not seen for twenty days. Henry knew from meeting Thompson on the Saskatchewan in August that he was heading for the pass above the North Saskatchewan and, as a colleague of some years, had two concerns: where Thompson was and how his brigade would bypass the Piegans. The latter problem had to be solved quickly because the Piegans turned up at Rocky Mountain House a few days later to ensure that the canoes did not attempt to proceed upstream.

Henry took care of the Piegans: on the night of October 11th he immobilized them with liquor to which he had added laudanum, and the voyageurs sped off upriver before dawn. The next morning Henry was astonished when, in company with three of his canoes, his cousin William appeared at Rocky Mountain House and announced that his chief was downriver on a tributary called the Brazeau. A day later Henry found Thompson "on top of a hill 300 feet above the water, where tall pines stood so thickly that I could not see his tent until we came within 10 yards of it". It seemed that Thompson had been occupying this spot for the better part of four weeks and was suffering from the effects of starvation, presumably because he still did not dare to use firearms and attract the attention of the Piegans. According to Henry, he persuaded Thompson to try to cross the mountains by a more northerly route — an old Indian trail that Henry had heard was somewhere near the headwaters of the Athabasca River.

On balance it seems likely that Thompson did lose his nerve and go into hiding. Regardless of what Alexander Henry says, Thompson admits that he sent William Henry and one of the hunters in search of the canoes "with positive orders not to fire a shot but in self defence", although he does not explain why he, the leader, stayed where he was. Upon their returning with the news that they had fired one shot as a recognition signal, his reaction was that "the Piegans would be on us very early in the morning" and he rode for his life, apparently with no further thought for the fate of his men. Then there is a time lag that implies a curious inactivity on Thompson's part. The *Narrative* accounts only for his arrival at "the foot of the Mountains" on October 13th, his flight across country on or about the 18th, and the discovery on or about the 19th that the canoes and the voyageurs were "forty miles below the Indians at a trading post lately deserted." In 1808 it took him from August 4th to October 31st to go from Rainy Lake House as far west as the upper Columbia. In 1810 he probably left the same supply point in late July but by October 19th or thereabouts was still only in the foothills of the Rocky Mountains; indeed, he and his twenty-four men did not reassemble with horses, goods, and supplies to *begin* to seek a more northerly pass until, as he himself states, the 29th of October.

As remarked earlier, Thompson's *Narrative* account of this

whole episode is barely three pages long. And it leaves even more untold than has so far been indicated. For example, Thompson does not say that his canoemen, thanks to Henry, escaped the Piegans and were able to make their way towards the headwaters of the North Saskatchewan, where he could have joined them by a circuitous route and proceeded on over the pass and down to the Columbia. For that matter he does not explain how he rejoined his men, simply remarking, again in that secretive plural way, "We therefore directed the men to proceed through the woods to the defiles of the mountains and bring down the horses to take the goods across the country to the Athabaska River, and on the 28th October they arrived with twenty-four horses . . ." According to Henry, he himself sent off a courier on the 12th of October to bring the canoes back and, on the 17th, redirected the voyageurs across country to join Thompson, having secured pack horses and an Indian guide for them. What all this amounts to is that one cannot believe everything that Thompson says if the circumstances in question do not redound to his credit. He seems to have been unable to admit making mistakes or to reveal personal failings. And he gives Alexander Henry absolutely no credit for all his help.

Curiously enough, some word of the Piegan incident may have got around in Thompson's lifetime. In 1837 he was engaged in survey work in the Muskoka region of Upper Canada (Ontario). One of his colleagues, Captain Francis H. Baddeley of the Royal Engineers, a geologist, remarks when writing to a friend that Thompson "is highly qualified for the duty in point of scientific and professional acquirements" but adds that "there are rumours abroad that Mr T is not trustworthy as to reporting of facts. This I mention without knowing what degree of credit to attach, although I must confess that there is something in his conversation which I do not like and which makes me suspect his candour."

If Thompson's actions in the September and October of 1810 are questionable, those for the winter of 1810-11 are clear. He made heroic efforts to resume and extend the Company's trading operations on the Pacific slope. To begin with he spent eleven weeks hauling several tons of supplies through heavily wooded, mountainous terrain, although the odds were against his finding a practicable route through to the Pacific slope.* He and Duncan McGillivray, searching in different directions, had not found one in the fall of 1800. In 1801, when he had accompanied James Hughes into the mountains, no way had been found through to the coast although they had had an Indian guide with them. Jaco Finlay found the pass above the North Saskatchewan in 1806-7, but only through the accident of meeting up with some Kootenays.

Thompson's many hardships began when he and his men were forced to spend the better part of four weeks hacking their way through thick brush and timber on their northwest course to the Athabasca River. Movement became much easier when they emerged onto frozen marshland and swamp near the river itself, but the intense cold, often as low as 30° below zero, steadily sapped their strength and made them tired and clumsy much of the time. What with the bitter weather and the continual need to hunt to supplement their food supplies, it was the 30th of December before they began to follow the broad valley of the Athabasca into the moun-

---

* While there are many passes within or across the Rocky Mountains, there are only four breaches in the 1000-mile length in Canada of this mountain barrier: four rail lines with highways alongside, one being next the Peace River, the only waterway that pierces the entire mountain chain.

tains. At this point most of the horses were so spent that the trade goods had to be transported by dog sleds hastily constructed out of logs. To make matters worse, game proved scarce, and Thompson, still low on provisions and reduced to slaughtering several horses in order to eke out food supplies, was forced to send some of his men back to Rocky Mountain House. About this time a few deserted and returned to the fur post, bluntly telling Alexander Henry that the condition of the men still with Thompson was "pitiful".

The weather remained well below zero as the party slogged on into ever deepening snow in which the dogs floundered and the sleds stuck time after time. Where the tributary of the Miette joins the Athabasca (just south of modern Jasper), Thompson had no option but to lighten the sleds and leave William Henry with the surplus goods. It was in this neighbourhood, too, that he turned loose the few remaining horses; some of his voyageurs had to shoulder the packs the horses had carried. Thirteen men and eight dog sleds laboured on south up the wide, wooded valley of the Athabasca for about another fifteen miles until their Indian guide halted and looked back to the northwest. After checking their position with that of a mighty peak (Mt Edith Cavell), which in later years came to be called "the Mountain of the Grand Crossing", he pointed the way up a frozen waterway (Whirlpool River) that came from the southwest out of a long mist-shrouded valley.

On January 8th, by which date they had trekked painfully but steadily up to the 5000-ft level through low clouds and swirling snow storms, Thompson noted what must have been chinook weather:

*We marched ten miles today; and as we advance we feel*

*In the middle distance is the lower valley of the Whirlpool River (Alta),
whose waters led David Thompson past the southeast spur of Mt Edith
Cavell (left middle ground), past Mt Evans (left foreground), and on up
to the Athabasca Pass. This photograph is a striking example of the
importance of waterways to fur traders travelling through the Rockies
or the mountainous Pacific Northwest. Whether frozen or free-running,
rivers were the only highways through these regions.*

*the mild weather from the Pacific Ocean. This morning at 7
a.m. Ther[mometer] +6, at 9 p.m. +22 . . .*

*January 9th. Ther +32. SE wind and snowed all day, which
made hauling very bad. We could proceed only four miles,
this partly up a brook and then over a steep high point with
dwarf pines. We had to take only half a load and return for
the rest. The snow is full seven feet deep, tho' firm and wet,
yet the dogs often sunk in it; but our snowshoes did [not]
sink more than three inches; and the weather so mild that the
snow is dropping from the trees and everything wet . . .*

By the morning of the 10th the temperature had dropped
back to 16°, but Thompson and his men were almost clear of
the timberline, and he sensed that they were very close to the
height of land. That night, a clear and brilliant one, he
walked a little way from the campfire and discovered that he
was in an immense cut in the mountains and on its western
edge. Far below he saw a dark ribbon of water that wound
towards him and then swung around in a big bend and moved
away towards the southwest. He guessed — correctly — that
this was the river he called the "Kootenae".

Thompson also found that he and his men were on top of
an icefield, part of the enormous glacier of "a clean fine
green colour" he could see less than a mile to the north.

*I returned and found part of my men with a pole of
twenty feet in length boring the snow to find the bottom. I
told them while we had good snowshoes, it was no matter to
us whether the snow was ten or one hundred feet deep. On
looking into the hole they had bored I was surprised to see
the colour of the sides of a beautiful blue; the surface was of
a very light colour, but as it descended the colour became*

*more deep and at the lowest point was of a blue, almost black.*

A day or two later, as his men and dog sleds stumbled and plunged through the deep snow and dense stands of timber on the steep western slopes of the Rocky Mountains, David Thompson was unaware that he was blazing a trail that many would follow. Largely because of the continual threat of pillage, if not of violence, from Piegans, the crossing he had just made (and, of course, surveyed) became a regular route of the Nor'Westers and, later, of the men from the Bay. Once time and money had been spent clearing a trail through the heavy timber on either side of the (Kane) glacier, traders and supplies poured over this pass, down the Wood River to the embarkation point at the big hairpin bend of the Columbia that became known as Canoe Encampment, and then made their way southeast into Kootenay or Salish country or southwest through what is now southern British Columbia and into the state of Washington. All of this was the great Inland Empire, the last frontier of the fur trade. The Nor'-Westers were to haul a wealth of furs over the pass until, in 1821, they were absorbed into the Hudson's Bay Company.

Crossing mountains in midwinter was just one of Thompson's difficulties. In addition to having to send one or two men back to Rocky Mountain House with messages on several occasions, some had deserted. They were probably worn out by the cold and their labours or perhaps they were panic-stricken by the silence and vague menace of the icy regions through which Thompson was leading them. Voyageurs were a superstitious breed, and those on this expedition were terrified at being in country reputed to be the home of a huge, hairy, monstrous-looking animal.

*Strange to say, here is a strong belief that the haunt of the mammoth is about this defile. I questioned several of the men. None could positively say they had seen him, but their belief I found firm and not to be shaken. I remarked to them that such an enormous heavy animal must leave indelible marks of his feet and his feeding. This they all acknowledged, and that they had never seen any marks of him and therefore could show me none. All I could say did not shake their belief in his existence.*

Their fears must have been greatly increased when, on one occasion, the party came across animal tracks, each as large as 14" x 8", that looked to have been made only six hours earlier. Thompson said that these were the marks of "a large old grizzled bear", a reasonable supposition, but the men "would have it to be a young mammoth." At any rate, by January 26th he and his party had come down alongside a raging stream (the Wood) he named Flat Heart, "from the men being dispirited", to where the northward-flowing Columbia curls around the northern end of the Selkirk Mountains and then rolls on to the southwest. That day he had no sooner sent three of his party back for supplies offloaded farther back along the trail than four others forsook him and he was left with only one man.

The next problem was transportation. Until spring came and the sap began to run in the birch trees, it was impossible to "raise" or strip birchbark with which to make canoes. And so Thompson patiently passed the weeks of February and early March hunting game and laying up stores of deer and moose meat or writing up his notes in a hut made from boards split from cedar trees. Building the hut must have involved a considerable expenditure of energy because he remarks that the axes he had were but two pounds in weight and that the cedars were from fifteen to thirty-six feet in girth and appeared to have six or eight sides. He noted that the smallest and scarcest tree was the white birch. The commonest and largest was the pine, eighteen to forty-two feet in girth, rising two hundred feet without a branch and topped with "a luxuriant head". Thompson describes the trees on the east side of the mountains as being small and with branches to the ground and says "there we were men, but on the west side we were pigmies".

He was rejoined in February by three voyageurs and an Indian guide, who arrived with two sled loads of goods and dried provisions. Prepared with their help to build canoes, Thompson examined the white birch all around for rind or bark

*without finding any thick enough to make a dish; such is the influence of a mild climate on the rind of the birch tree. We had to turn our thoughts to some other material, and cedar wood being the lightest and most pliable for a canoe, we split out thin boards of cedar wood of about six inches in breadth and builded a canoe of twenty-five feet in length by fifty inches in breadth, of the same form of a common canoe, using cedar boards instead of birch rind, which proved to be equally light and much stronger than birch rind. The greatest difficulty we had was sewing the boards to each round the timbers. As we had no nails, we had to make use of the fine roots of the pine . . .*

Thompson still did not know that the river to which he and his men carried their cedar canoe was the Columbia. He was fairly certain that it was the "Kootenae" and decided to ascend it and go down via "McGillivray's River" (the modern

Kootenay) to the Salish country and pick up reinforcements and supplies. For one thing, he feared that his party was too small and too poorly armed to venture down a river he assumed led to the Pacific but which he also assumed passed through regions inhabited by many Indian groups. For another, he considered that he had far too few trade goods with which to bribe his way past hostile natives, and as it happened he had only about 200 pounds of provisions with which to feed himself and his companions if they should fail to find game to supplement these rations.

When Thompson and his men set off upstream on April 17th, it was almost nine months since he had left Rainy Lake House with orders to go to the mouth of the Columbia and oppose the Pacific Fur Company. For much of this time he had been beset by personal fears and plagued by problems of supply, transportation, and labour. But he had an iron will and great stamina and was able to lead his handful of men several hundred miles south over rivers dangerously swollen with spring runoff. It rained often and heavily, and they were nearly always cold and wet to the skin. It took them 27 days just to get to the portage at the head of the Columbia, principally because they had to cross a frozen lake (Kinbasket) at one point and could only do so by building a sled and hauling their canoe across the ice. After paddling all the way down to the southern bend of the Kootenay, it was the end of May before they had obtained horses and ridden overland to Salish House on the Clark Fork River in Montana. Here Thompson learned of the recent construction of a new western post, Spokane House, built by the men of his Department late in 1810 or early in 1811 at the junction of the Spokane and Little Spokane Rivers, about ten miles northwest of the present city of Spokane, Washington. He promptly had his men construct another cedar canoe and then led them west.

On June 14th Thompson paused at Spokane House long enough to borrow horses before going north along an old Indian trail to "Ilthkoyape Falls" (Kettle Falls), a river rendezvous for many inhabitants of the region, where he had his men make yet another cedar canoe. He now calculated that he was not far from the mouth of the Columbia and was fairly certain that he was on the Columbia itself. He worked out the position of Kettle Falls as "48° .38' .7" N and 117° .48' .49" W "; following its discovery in 1792 by Captain Robert Gray of the American merchant ship *Columbia*, the mouth of the river was known to be at 46° 20' N and 124° W.

Thompson set out downstream on July 3rd, writing in his journal that "We set off on a voyage down the Columbia River to explore this river in order to open out a passage for the interior trade with the Pacific Ocean." The voyage was unhurried and broken by several halts to talk with natives encamped along or near the banks and induce them to trap for furs. By means of interpreters, he carefully explained what they could gain for themselves by trading with his Company. Many of these conversations were accompanied by the ritual of pipe smoking, and Thompson found himself forced to join in and to hand out tobacco twist by the yard. Despite his dislike of smoking, he was willing to take a pipe if it would help to make his return upriver less risky by cementing friendly relations with the Indians.

On July 10th he heard from Indians of "the American ship's arrival" and knew he was now close to his destination. Four days later the presence of seals playing in the river confirmed that he was very near salt water. The next day, July 15th, Thompson at last caught sight of the Pacific,

*which to me was a great pleasure, but my men seemed
disappointed. They had been accustomed to the boundless
horizon of the great lakes of Canada and their high rolling
waves. From the ocean they expected a more boundless view,
a something beyond the power of their senses which they
could not describe; and my informing them that directly
opposite to us, at the distance of five thousand miles, was the
empire of Japan added nothing to their ideas . . .*

On the south bank of the Columbia estuary he spotted the
four log huts that comprised Fort Astoria, the newly built
trading post of the Pacific Fur Company. One of the Astorians, Gabriel Franchère, a French Canadian, has described
Thompson's approach:

*Toward midday we saw a large canoe with a flag displayed
at her stern rounding the point we called Tongue Point. The
flag she bore was the British, and her crew was composed of
eight Canadian boatmen or voyageurs. A well-dressed man,
who appeared to be the commander, was the first to leap
ashore.*[4]

The head of the Columbia Department was politely received
by Messrs Duncan McDougall and David Stuart, the fort's
joint commanders and lately clerks in the North West Company.

Characteristically, Thompson just stayed a few days in
order to rest his men and to repair the canoe: he was anxious
to be off again to expand his Department's trading operations
and deprive the Astorians of as many customers as possible.
On his return journey up the Columbia to Kettle Falls he
again assured many groups of Indians that he would return to
trade with them and handed out more gifts of tobacco. By
mid-August he was back at Spokane House, asking the natives

of the area to bring in a good harvest of furs because he was off to the mountains for a supply of trade goods. Then he returned to Kettle Falls, pausing there long enough to build a canoe and to send word to Finan McDonald at Kullyspell House to keep the Flatheads and their allies well supplied with ammunition and thus secure the southeastern frontier of the Department from Piegan raids. By September 2nd he was on his way to collect his merchandise and he travelled up the Columbia in the hope that it would take him to the Rocky Mountains.

The *Narrative* lacks any description of his journey up this section of the river, but Thompson's journals make it clear that he pushed his men hard. On September 4th he crossed the 49th parallel and camped for the night just a little north of the present town of Trail, B.C. About noon on the following day they passed the entry into the Columbia of the Kootenay River and stopped off for the night near the site of Castlegar. Six days later he had traversed the beautiful Arrow lakes and was a mile or two north of modern Revelstoke, very pleased by calculations that confirmed that he was heading for the mountains. Despite the strong current and the steady rise in elevation of the river, he continued to rouse his men in the early hours of the morning and kept them paddling until evening. About noon on the 18th he arrived at the cedar hut he had built close to where the Canoe and Wood Rivers enter the Columbia.

Thompson must have been elated. He had found the river Fraser had sought in vain and the navigable waterway to the Pacific that Mackenzie had dreamed of discovering. Moreover, the Columbia led directly to and from Spokane House, from which goods and furs could be exchanged with the posts in the Salish country and from which trade could be carried on with the tribes of the lower Columbia, a region that became known to history as the Oregon Territory. In effect, Thompson had discovered the Pacific-coast equivalent of the Saskatchewan, the great highway of the plains.

For the rest of 1811 Thompson simply tied up a few loose ends and let others continue the work he had begun. He crossed over into the valley of the Athabasca, picked up the goods left at William Henry's camp on the Miette, and returned with them to Kettle Falls. He rode east to Salish House on the Clark Fork River and, finding that it had fallen into disuse, repaired it in anticipation of renewed trading activities. Here he heard from local Indians that a Piegan war party had been looking for him upstream, but this bad news was offset a few days later when eighteen men arrived from Rainy Lake House with 1200 pounds of merchandise. Thompson was equally pleased to learn about this time that his second-in-command, Finan McDonald, was drumming up business among the Flatheads living southeast of Salish House.

Early in March 1812 Thompson set out for Fort William and his long-delayed retirement in the east. It had been a good trading season, and his party travelled with 122 ninety-pound packs of furs. Thus he initiated in person the trade route up the Columbia and over the Athabasca Pass. Picking up his family en route at Winnipeg House, he arrived at the Rendezvous on July 12th. That he received a warm welcome from his fellow partners is shown by an entry in the minutes of the annual meeting held on July 18th:

*A resolve entered into that Mr David Thompson now going down on rotation shall be allowed his full share of the profits for three years and one hundred pounds besides; that he is to finish his charts, maps &c. and deliver them to the agents in*

*that time, after which he is to be considered as a retired*
*partner and enjoy the profits of one hundredth for seven*
*years. The hundred per annum is meant for compensation for*
*making use of his own instruments &c. &c. and for furnishing*
*him with implements for drawing, writing, &c.*[5]

According to Company regulations, in order to continue to
hold his full share in the "concern" a partner had either to
winter in the interior or retire for one year in rotation.
Thompson's notoriously thrifty, if not miserly, colleagues
voted him his full share of the profits for *three* years. This
was ample evidence of the high regard in which they held him
and how much they appreciated his efforts and achievements
in fifteen years of service.

Thompson settled in Terrebonne near Montreal. Here he
achieved his ambition to chart western North America by
producing his huge "MAP OF THE NORTH-WEST TER-
RITORY". It showed the principal rivers, lakes, portages,
mountain peaks, and passes of that portion of the continent
between Hudson Bay and the Pacific Ocean, and from the
Great Lakes and the Columbia River in the south to Lake
Athabasca on the north; it also revealed the locations of the
74 Company posts then in existence.

In 1784 (the year Thompson arrived at York Factory), when
the great map of the world accompanying the account of
Captain Cook's third voyage was published, almost the whole
of the North American continent north and west of Lake
Winnipeg appeared as a complete blank. With the exception
of the extreme north and northwestern reaches of the continent, Thompson filled in this immense blank in the course of
some 50,000 miles of travel by canoe, on horseback, and on

foot. His success in charting with such general accuracy the principal features of the regions he travelled establishes him as the greatest land geographer of North America. With the possible exception of the *Narrative*, the map is his greatest achievement. It hung in the great hall of Fort William until 1821 when the North West Company was absorbed into the Hudson's Bay Company. Then the map vanished, to turn up again in government archives as inexplicably as it had disappeared from the Rendezvous.

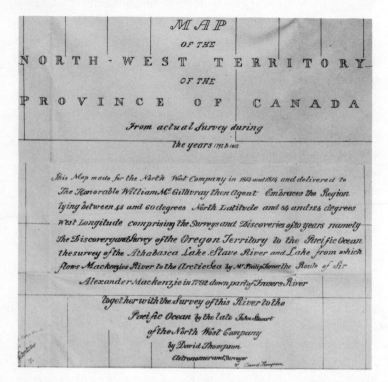

# Epilogue

In the years 1816-26 Thompson achieved some recognition when he acted as "Astronomer and Surveyor to the British Boundary Commission". On behalf of the British government he surveyed and mapped the Canada-U.S. boundary line from St Regis in Lower Canada (Quebec) to the northwest angle of the Lake of the Woods, today the junction of the boundaries of Ontario, Manitoba, and Minnesota. Thereafter he suffered a steady series of misfortunes.

At one point Thompson left Terrebonne and settled in Williamstown in Glengarry County, Upper Canada (Ontario), where he bought a substantial house and some eighty acres of land. There he set up some of his sons in business, but their ventures failed and he was obliged to pay off all their debts. Even money he made in the 1830s surveying for government agencies or for private companies in the Muskoka region of Upper Canada, in the eastern townships of Lower Canada, and in Montreal itself could not make up for these considerable losses. He was even forced to sell his Williamstown property. Some time in the 1840s Thompson began to write the *Narrative* in order to support himself and his family on whatever he could get for it. (He hoped to receive $30 a month as a subsidy from "a few gentlemen" who would

"form a Company" and "be entitled to and shall have half
the net profits of the publication.") But he was no business-
man, and despite the care he took with his writing — much of
the *Narrative* was written at least twice — it was neither
subsidized nor printed in his lifetime. Thompson suffered
intermittent attacks of glaucoma and was actually blind at
various times throughout the last nine years of his life.
During that period he and his wife were totally dependent
upon the charity of a son-in-law. Even then he was obliged
to sell some of his clothing and his precious instruments to
procure money for food. David Thompson died early in 1857
in circumstances of extreme poverty.

Obscurity surrounded Thompson even after death. The
wilderness trail by which he had first found a way to the
Columbia was called Howse Pass after an HBC trader of
Thompson's day. The defile in the ice-encased heights where
he made his magnificent crossing in 1811 remained known as
the Athabasca Pass. (The Thompson Pass immediately south
of the Columbia Icefield is named for C. S. Thompson, the
alpinist, who crossed over here in 1900.) While he was still an
HBC man, his notebooks and maps were passed by the
Company to Aron Arrowsmith, the first of a famous family
of cartographers in London, who incorporated their information in his maps of British North America, information for
which the Company was credited. Similarly Arrowsmith's
revisions of 1802, 1811, and 1814 of his map of North
America published in 1795 were based on details of Thompson's work passed on to him by the North West Company.
Again no acknowledgement of Thompson was ever made.
The fur trade declined, and settlers moved into the Oregon
Territory, but Thompson had no mention in early histories of
the region. Only a secondary river winding its way to the

mountains of the north Pacific coast bore his name.

David Thompson might have remained a mere footnote to history had it not been for the curiosity of a Canadian geologist. During the 1880s Joseph B. Tyrrell was travelling in and near the Rocky Mountains as a member of the Geological Survey of Canada and became intrigued by the general accuracy of the main features of the old government maps he was using. After some inquiry Tyrrell was told that a large map and several notebooks in the files of the Crown Lands Department of the Province of Ontario were the sources of these maps. In the Department he found a dusty collection of thirty-nine journals, eleven books of field notes, and a yellowing map of the western half of North America between the 45th and 60th parallels, 10' 3 1/2" by 6' 6" in extent and on a scale of fifteen miles to the inch.

After he had studied the journals and found them to be Thompson's, Tyrrell published *A Brief Narrative of the Journeys of David Thompson in North-Western America.* Sometime later he was approached by Charles Lindsey, the registrar of deeds for Toronto, who revealed that one of Thompson's sons had sold him the manuscript of his father's *Narrative.* Lindsey offered it for Tyrrell's inspection. Some years later he purchased the manuscript and accepted an offer to have it edited and published under the auspices of the Champlain Society. As Tyrrell remarks in the Preface to his edition of the *Narrative:*

*Between the years 1883 and 1898, when engaged on the staff of the Geological Survey of Canada, it fell to my lot to carry on exploration in canoes, on horseback, and on foot, over many of the routes which had been surveyed and explored by David Thompson a century before, to survey the rivers that he had surveyed, to measure the portages on which he had walked, to cross the plains and mountains on the trails which he had travelled, to camp on his old camping grounds, and to take astronomical observations on the same places where he had taken them. Everywhere his work was found to be of the highest order, considering the means and facilities at his disposal, and as my knowledge of his achievements widened, my admiration for this fur-trading geographer increased, and in order to show my appreciation of the splendid work which he did I decided to offer this narrative to the public.*

We are all in Tyrrell's debt.

# Notes

[1] Wallace, W. S., *Documents Relating to the North West Company*, Toronto, The Champlain Society, 1934. Introduction.

[2] McKenny, Thomas L., *Sketches of a Tour to the Lakes, of the Character and Customs of the Chippeway Indians and of Incidents Connected with the Treaty of Fond Du Lac*, Baltimore, 1827.

[3] Cox, Ross, *Adventures on the Columbia River: including the narrative of a residence of six years on the western side of the Rocky Mountains, among various tribes of Indians hitherto unknown, together with a journey across the American continent*, London, 1831.

[4] Franchère, G., *Narrative of a voyage to the northwest coast of America in the years 1811, 1812, 1813 and 1814,* translated and edited by J. V. Huntington, New York, 1854.

[5] Wallace, W. S., *Documents Relating to the North West Company*, Toronto, The Champlain Society, 1934.

# Indian Groups

## CHIPEWYANS

Several bands of forest-dwelling Athapaskan-speaking Indians whose home was Churchill River country. They are supposed to have received their names from a Cree term meaning "Pointed Skins", a term that referred to the form in which the Chipewyans dried their beaver skins. The Chipewyans were nomadic hunters, and there is a long history of border wars between Chipewyan and Cree.

## CREES

The name comes from "Cris", a shortened form of the French term Kristinaux or Kristineaux. By the late eighteenth century the Cree nation had increased in numbers, and many bands, in search of beaver, moved westward from the original homeland of forest and lake immediately south of Hudson Bay to inhabit large portions of what are now northwestern Ontario, northern Manitoba and Saskatchewan, and northeastern Alberta. This expansion led to the formation of two main divisions: the Plains Cree and the Woodland Cree. The former quickly adopted the horse and the buffalo hunt. The latter continued to seek beaver.

## FLATHEADS

Indians of the Salishan linguistic stock, also known as the Salish Indians. These people never practised head flattening, but the Columbia River tribes who did, compressing the front parts of their heads to create a pointed appearance, referred to the Salish as, by contrast, flat heads. Like the Kootenays, the Salish rode horses and hunted buffalo and were thus considered enemies by the Piegans and other Blackfoot bands.

## KOOTENAYS

The Kootenays (or Kootenaes or Kutenai or Kutenais) were a distinct linguistic group with two main divisions: the Upper Kootenays of the upper Columbia River region and the Lower Kootenays of the lower Kootenay River. Originally plains dwellers, these Indians had been driven west by the Piegans once the latter had obtained firearms from traders. However, in Thompson's time the Upper Kootenays still occasionally journeyed to the prairies to hunt buffalo and to barter furs.

## NOOTKAS

The Nootkas of the west coast of Vancouver Island and the Kwakiutls of the east coast and of the neighbouring mainland were the two main divisions of a linguistic group known as the Wakashan Indians. A seafaring people, the Nootkas were, in particular, seal and whale hunters.

## OJIBWAYS

The Ojibwa or Ojibway, whose name was garbled into Chippewa or Chippeway by fur traders, belonged to the huge linguistic group of Algonkian-speaking Indians and

were basically a hunting and fishing people. The Lake
Superior Ojibwa were excellent canoe builders and, as
trappers and middlemen, had been of great help to the
French as the fur trade moved over the prairies and into
the western forests.

## PIEGANS

The Piegans (pronounced Pay-gans), the Bloods, and the
Blackfoot, often referred to collectively as the Blackfoot
or Blackfeet, were tribes belonging to the same linguistic
group. In Thompson's time they roamed the plains
country of what is now southern Alberta and Montana in
search of the buffalo, which provided them with food,
clothing, and their conical tents or tipis of hide; they
cheerfully raided other Indian groups in order to steal their
horses. The name Blackfoot refers to their moccasins,
either because these were painted black or were blackened
by the ashes of prairie grass fires. Piegan comes from a
word meaning "poor robes", but its significance, as with
the name Blood, is unknown owing to several contra-
dictory legends.

## SIOUX

These were the Dakota Sioux, a group of Siouan-speaking
Indians. Other members of the Dakota family were the
Mandans of what is now North Dakota, the Crows of the
upper Missouri River, and the Tetons and Yanktons west
of the Missouri. The Tetons, the main body of the Dakota
and the famous Sioux of Western novels and movies, were
a particularly fierce, disciplined people. General George
Crook, a famous American cavalryman and an Indian-
fighter of no mean repute, once described them as "the
finest light cavalry in the world".

# Biographical Sidelights

JACQUES RAPHAEL FINLAY (d. 1828) — variously referred to as Joco, Jacco, Jacko, Jaccot, or Jacko — was the halfbreed son of an unknown Indian woman and the James Finlay who was trading on the Saskatchewan as early as 1768. Jaco is mentioned by John McDonald of Garth in his reminiscences as "a man of courage" when relating the defence of the North West Company post on the "Bow" (South Saskatchewan) River against the Blackfoot in 1794. He was with David Thompson at Rocky Mountain House and worked on the Saskatchewan at various times during the period 1800-6 as a Nor'Wester guide, interpreter, and hunter.

Finlay was one of the first of those individuals known to history as the "mountain men" — highly independent characters who chose to live in the wilds of the Pacific Northwest, trapping and trading on their own and occasionally acting for fur companies as scouts and interpreters, and at a later date as wagon-train guides for groups of pioneers. He accompanied Thompson on his second (1809) journey into Montana and seems to have helped Finan McDonald to build Spokane House in 1810 or 1811. Thereafter he is mentioned in the journals of various persons travelling in the Northwest. Even

Governor Simpson of the Hudson's Bay Company, in an account of a journey to Fort George (originally Astoria), records meeting Jaco near the Athabasca Pass late in 1824. The Jocko River, a tributary of the Flathead River in Montana, was named for Finlay.


SAMUEL HEARNE (1745-92) was born in London, England. A bit of a wild boy at school, his family packed him off to the Royal Navy, where he saw plenty of action as a midshipman. He joined the Hudson's Bay Company in 1766, serving initially as a mate on the Company's whaling vessels, but became bored and two years later sought inland service. In the course of northward exploration he discovered the Coppermine River and followed it to the Arctic Ocean, returning to the Bay in a great arc that included Great Slave Lake. Hearne's story of his travels and explorations, *A Journey from Prince of Wales's Fort, in Hudson's Bay, to the Northern Ocean . . . in the years 1769, 1770,1771,1772*, is a classic account of the techniques of wilderness exploration and survival. Editions of this were prepared for the Champlain Society by J. B. Tyrrell in 1911 and by R. Glover in 1958. Tyrrell also edited for the Society *The Journals of Samuel Hearne and Philip Turnor between the years 1774 and 1792* (1934).

Hearne became governor of Fort Prince of Wales in 1775 and, after it was reduced by a French naval force, in 1783 was given command of the fort's replacement, Churchill Factory, remaining in charge there until his retirement in 1787. Thompson, of course, served under Hearne in 1783-4.

In his *Narrative*, Thompson makes a number of complimentary remarks about Hearne. However, Thompson also implies, somewhat maliciously and quite incorrectly, several unfavourable characteristics, which include cowardice.

ALEXANDER HENRY the Younger (d.1814), the nephew of his famous namesake, joined the North West Company about 1794, was made a partner in 1802, and began his wintering duties in the Red River Department. He served in 1808-13 in the Saskatchewan Department, and for one year in the Columbia Department. He was drowned at the mouth of the Columbia River when a canoe capsized.

Henry was a restless character who liked to get away from his business duties whenever he could and wander about the prairies, usually accompanied by his unofficial second-in-command, a 200-pound Negro voyageur called Pierre Bonga, and a huge black hound, part Newfoundland dog and part wolf. From 1799 until the night before his death, Henry made daily journal entries in which he noted the details of life as he experienced and witnessed it in the West. His writings are a series of vivid sidelights on the fur trade, but even more so of the natural history of the prairies, albeit some of his views of Indians are less than sympathetic. Henry's journals contain many references to David Thompson, whom he often encountered during the latter's journeys to and from the Columbia Department.

The original Henry journals have never been found, but a transcript of them, made by a George Coventry about 1824, is now preserved in the Public Archives of Canada, Ottawa. Walter O'Meara's book, *The Savage Country* (Houghton Mifflin, 1960), is a colourful retelling of various episodes in Henry's life.

FINAN MCDONALD (1782-1851) was born in Scotland but

grew up in the Glengarry district of Upper Canada, to which his family immigrated sometime about 1786. In 1804 he became a Nor'Wester and spent a great deal of time assisting David Thompson to organize the Columbia Department. In particular, McDonald helped build Kootanae House, established the first trading post in the present state of Montana, was in charge of Kullyspell House (Idaho), the first permanent trading centre in the Inland Empire, and built Spokane House (Washington). Until he retired to Glengarry County in 1826, much of his time in the Pacific Northwest was spent in the Columbia valley, mainly at the Salish and Spokane posts. McDonald took to the Salish way of life with gusto. He married the daughter of a Pend Oreille chief, lived with the Salish, rode with them on their buffalo hunts, and on at least one occasion joined them in battling their ancient enemy, the Blackfoot.

In his *Adventures on the Columbia River* (London, 1832), Ross Cox, a member of Astor's Pacific Fur Company, describes McDonald's striking appearance: "in height he was six feet four inches, with broad shoulders, large bushy whiskers, and red hair, which for some years had not felt the scissors, and which sometimes falling over his face and shoulders gave to his countenance a wild and uncouth appearance." He adds, "McDonald was a most extraordinary and original character. To the gentleness of a lamb he united the courage of a lion. He was especially affectionate to men of small size, whether equals or inferiors, and would stand their bantering with the utmost good-humour: but if any man approaching his own altitude presumed to encroach too far on his good-nature, a lowering look and distended nostrils warned the intruder of an approaching eruption."

JOHN MCDONALD OF GARTH (1774? — 1860), so called to distinguish him from the many other John McDonalds in the fur trade, was born in Scotland and immigrated to North America in 1791 to join the "concern". He spent several years in the Saskatchewan country, becoming a partner of the North West Company in 1800. When the Company used the excuse of the War of 1812 to take over Astor's post on the Columbia, McDonald was one of a group of Nor'Westers present aboard the sloop-of-war, *Raccoon*, on December 12th, 1813, when Fort Astoria surrendered and the establishment was rechristened Fort George.

Perhaps because he was small in stature and the possessor of an arm deformed in a childhood accident, McDonald displayed great energy and hardihood. His department was renowned for its aggressive activities, and on one occasion McDonald did not scruple to secure the temporary friendship of the Piegans by joining them on one of their horse-stealing raids. Oddly enough he was one of the few North West Company partners to deal amicably with the first Selkirk settlers.

McDonald retired to Glengarry County, Upper Canada, in 1816. His *Autobiographical Notes, 1791-1816,* published in part in L. R. Masson's *Les Bourgeois de la Compagnie du Nord-Ouest* (Quebec, 1889-90) is interesting source material. However his *Notes* are occasionally as unreliable as parts of Thompson's *Narrative,* probably because both men were quite old by the time they came to put pen to paper and memory had distorted their views of events and contemporaries.

WILLIAM MCGILLIVRAY (1764 — 1825) was born in Scotland and immigrated to North America at the age of twenty to become a clerk in the North West Company. His being made a partner six years later was partly owing to the patronage and help of his uncle Simon McTavish, the dominant figure in Company councils. After the death of McTavish in 1804, McGillivray in effect took over the leadership of the individual fur concerns comprising the Company and managed their affairs ably. However he was quite ruthless in the pursuit of profits, and his private approval of the massacre of certain Selkirk settlers in 1816 was only another example of the Mafia-like tactics employed from time to time by the directorate of the North West Company.

Personally McGillivray was a tall, handsome, red-haired Highlander, markedly courteous to all and thus quite an exception to the usual run of partners and agents, whose brute arrogance towards their employees was notorious even in a caste-conscious society and age. Where many of the partners had no patience with exploration, McGillivray was shrewd enough to foresee the potential return in furs and money, hence his encouragement of Thompson's survey work for the Company. At a later date it was this same shrewdness that enabled McGillivray to appreciate the wisdom of merging with the Hudson's Bay Company. Together with his brother Simon, who looked after the London interests of the "concern", he played a notable part in effecting this union.

Little is known about MALCOLM (MALCHOM) ROSS (1755? -1799). He is thought to have been a native of the Orkney Islands. In 1774 he was engaged by the Hudson's Bay Company as a "labourer" and sent to York Factory. Philip Turnor says of Ross that he was "an excellent Servant and a Good Canoe Man", steady and careful, and speaks of his having an excellent understanding of the Cree and Chipewyan languages and commanding a great affection from these Indians.

Thompson's sudden departure in 1797 forced Ross to postpone his retirement and continue as "Master to the Northward". The following year he went to England to appeal directly to the HBC directors to support expansion into the Athabasca country, where, in company with Turnor, he had seen the great wealth of furs to be gained. Late in 1799, while travelling inland from Churchill Factory, Ross was drowned in a rapid.

PHILIP TURNOR (1751? -1800) was the first man to be employed by the Hudson's Bay Company in the sole capacity of surveyor. Nothing is known of his earliest years except that he came from Middlesex, England, and was recommended to the Company by the "Mathematical Master" of Christ's Hospital, the famous charity school, although Turnor's name is not in the school's records as having been a pupil there. However, he must have been a young man who had achieved some success and standing because a letter of 13 May, 1778 from the Governor and Committee of the Company introducing him to Humphry Marten, Chief at York Factory, contains a strong recommendation:

*Being very desirous to have the Longitude and Latitude of our several Factories ascertained and also of our Inland Settlements, and their respective Distances from one another ... We have engaged Mr Philip Turnor under the Title of Inland Surveyor for Three Years at £50 a year. He is to mess at your Table and also at the Tables of our other Chiefs during his stay at each Factory, and to be accommodated in the best manner possible for his several Journeys.*

Although Turnor actually spent some time as a trader, the bulk of his service was spent exploring and surveying, as far south as Lake Superior, westward along the Saskatchewan and Churchill Rivers, and northwest into the lower reaches of the Athabasca region. In the course of the winter (1789-90) he spent at Cumberland House, he not only tutored David Thompson but instructed another youth, Peter Fidler (1769-1822), who became an HBC surveyor of note. After the council at York rejected Turnor's proposal in 1792 that he return to Athabasca and establish a permanent post, he left North America and was employed for some years making maps in Company headquarters at London.

The survey maps and charts that the Company supplied to Aron Arrowsmith for his first map of North America were the work of Philip Turnor and were acknowledged by Arrowsmith. Information on Turnor is available in *The Journals of Samuel Hearne and Philip Turnor between the years 1774 and 1792,* edited by J. B. Tyrrell for the Champlain Society in 1934.

# Bibliography

Listed below are two groups of books. The first contains primary sources for Thompson's life and writings. The reader is advised to refer in particular to *David Thompson's Narrative 1784-1812*, edited with an introduction and notes by Richard Glover and published in 1962 by the Champlain Society*. Unlike Tyrrell's 1916 edition of the *Narrative*, this book contains a quite lengthy (and very readable) introduction to Thompson and his times. In addition, Professor Glover has retained Tyrrell's year-by-year itinerary of Thompson's travels in the West and many helpful footnotes that appeared in the 1916 edition; Glover has also appended a number of critical notes of his own. Reading introductions and footnotes may not be everyone's cup of tea, but these features of the 1962 edition are packed with information and opinion vital to any appreciation of Thompson and his achievements.

---

* The Society publishes editions of historical journals and collections of documents relating to the history of Canada. With the exception of its Ontario Series (obtainable from the University of Toronto Press), the Society does not make its publications available to non-members. However, the Greenwood Reprint Corporation of New York City (currently represented in Canada by Methuen Publications, 2330 Midland Ave., Scarborough, Ont.) has so far reprinted a facsimile edition of each of the first thirty-six volumes (1907-1958) published by the Champlain Society. Thus, for example, one can purchase or request a library to purchase (or borrow) W. Stewart Wallace's *Documents Relating to the North West Company* and Tyrrell's edition of the *Narrative*.

The second group contains two biographies of Thompson — published in 1928 and 1955 — and books on the fur trade, exploration of the continent, and the North American Indian. The literature on each of these subjects is considerable. I have chosen to draw the reader's attention to a selection of valuable recent studies and several older books that by reason of their lasting importance or popularity can be confidently recommended. An asterisk indicates a paperback edition.

The reader is also advised to consult historical atlases or maps, but with caution. Several examples of errors will suffice. The massive *Atlas of Canada* issued in 1957 by the Geographical Branch of the federal Department of Mines and Technical Surveys depicts Thompson's mountain journeys very carefully but fails to show that he travelled all the way to the mouth of the Columbia. The 1956 edition of the *British Columbia Atlas of Resources* shows him only on upper Columbia waters, and the 1960 edition of Kerr's *A Historical Atlas of Canada* does not indicate that he travelled the whole of the Columbia, including the great northern loop it makes on its way down to the international border. The *Atlas* also fails to delineate his 1811 crossing, although the Athabasca Pass is identified.

Coues, Elliott, ed., *New Light on the Early History of the Greater Northwest* [the journals of Alexander Henry, the Younger, 1799-1814 and collateral information from David Thompson's journals, edited with copious critical commentary] 3 vols., New York, 1897.

Glover, R., ed., *David Thompson's Narrative 1784-1812,* Toronto, The Champlain Society, 1962.

Hopwood, V. G., ed., *David Thompson Travels in Western North America 1784-1812*, Toronto, Macmillan, 1971.

Murray, Florence B., ed., *Muskoka and Haliburton 1615-1875: A Collection of Documents,* Toronto, The Champlain Society, 1963 [which contains some material by and about Thompson and his survey work between Lake Huron and the Ottawa River].

Tyrrell, J. B., ed., *David Thompson's Narrative of His Explorations in Western America 1784-1812,* Toronto, The Champlain Society, 1916.

Wallace, W. Stewart, ed., *Documents Relating to the North West Company,* Toronto, The Champlain Society, 1934.

White, M. Catherine, ed., *David Thompson's Journals relating to Montana and Adjacent Regions 1808-1812,* Montana State University, 1950.

---

Campbell, Marjorie W., *The Nor'Westers: the fight for the fur trade* (Great Stories of Canada No. 4.), Toronto, Macmillan, 1954.

Campbell, Marjorie W., *The Saskatchewan,* *Toronto, Clarke, Irwin, 1950.

Campbell, Marjorie W., *The North West Company*, Toronto Macmillan, 1957.

Cochrane, Charles N., *David Thompson the Explorer,* Toronto, Macmillan, 1928.

Dryden, Cecil, ed., *Up the Columbia for Furs*, Caldwell Idaho, Caxton Printers, Ltd., 1949 [a retelling of Ross Cox, *Adventures on the Columbia River* and Alexander Ross, *Fur Hunters of the Far West*].

Fraser, Esther, *The Canadian Rockies: Early Travels and Explorations,* Edmonton, M. G. Hurtig Ltd., 1969

Innis, Harold, *The Fur Trade in Canada,* * rev. ed., University of Toronto Press, 1956.

Jenness, Diamond, *The Indians of Canada,* 7th ed., Ottawa, The Queen's Printer, 1967

Josephy, Alvin M., Jr., *The Indian Heritage of America,* * New York, Bantam Books, 1969.

MacKay, Douglas, *The Honourable Company: a history of the Hudson's Bay Company,* rev. ed., Toronto, McClelland & Stewart, 1949.

MacLennan, Hugh, *Seven Rivers of Canada* [the Mackenzie, St Lawrence, Ottawa, Red, Saskatchewan, Fraser, St John] Toronto, Macmillan, 1963.

Morse, Eric W., *Fur Trade Canoe Routes of Canada/Then and Now,* Ottawa, Queen's Printer, 1969.

Nute, Grace L., *The Voyageur,* reprint edition, St Paul, Minnesota Historical Society, 1955.

O'Meara, Walter, *The Savage Country,* Boston, Houghton Mifflin, 1960.

Rich, E. E., *The Fur Trade and The Northwest to 1857,* Toronto. McClelland & Stewart, 1967.

Rich, E. E., *Montreal and the Fur Trade,* McGill University Press, 1966.

Thomson, Don W., *Men and Meridians: The History of Surveying and Mapping in Canada, Volume I Prior to 1867,* Ottawa, The Queen's Printer, 1966.

Wallace, W. Stewart, *By Star and Compass,* 2nd ed., Toronto, The Ryerson Press, 1953.

Warkentin, John, *The Western Interior of Canada: A Record of Geographical Discovery 1612-1917,* * Toronto, McClelland & Stewart, 1964.

Wood, Kerry, *The Map-Maker: the story of David Thompson*, (Great Stories of Canada No. 7), Toronto, Macmillan, 1955.

# INDEX

*Collective entries have been made as follows:*
*fur depots and posts; Indians; lakes; rivers.*